Lit

REASON IN MADNESS

CRITICAL ESSAYS

REASON IN MADNESS

CRITICAL ESSAYS

by Allen Tate

Essay Index Reprint Series

 BOOKS FOR LIBRARIES PRESS
FREEPORT, NEW YORK

LIBRARY OF CONGRESS CATALOG CARD NUMBER:
68-26479

PRINTED IN THE UNITED STATES OF AMERICA

LEAR.   *Get thee glass eyes,*
And, like the scurvy politician, seem
To see the things thou dost not. Now,
   now, now, now,
Pull off my boots; harder, harder: so.
EDGAR. *O, matter and impertinency mixed!*
Reason in madness!

To Andrew and Edna Lytle

PREFACE

THE ESSAYS collected here were written either for an occasion or upon assignment from an editor. Only one, "Literature as Knowledge," has been written specially for this book. Every essayist—and I distinguish the essayist from the systematic literary critic—must be grateful to his editors, as I am grateful for suggestions that led to the writing of all but three of these essays.

The reader will expect to see here only the consistency of a point of view. I hope that he will not be disappointed if he does not find it. Yet I believe that all the essays are on one theme: a deep illness of the modern mind. I place it in the mind because that is the level at which I am interested in it. At any rate the mind is the dark center from which one may see coming the darkness gathering outside us. The late W. B. Yeats had for it a beautiful phrase, "the mad abstract dark," and we are all in it together.

Few of the questions which have agitated what used to be called the "press" in the five years since the first of the papers was written, appear in this book. There are war and democracy, which are only casually mentioned. Certain features of the present war may be unique in the history of war, and if they are they may also be a symptom of our peculiar illness. What those features are this is not the place to say; yet our limitation of the whole human problem to the narrow scope of the political problem is obviously one of them. We are justified in saving democracy if democracy can save something else which will support it. That "something else," which we name with peril, so great is our distress, hovers round the periphery of these essays. Unless we consider it, everything we write will look, after a generation, when the historical irony becomes visible, like another tale of a tub.

Every writer writes within a convention which he picks up from someone else or invents for himself. The convention of this book is the attack. It asks of people who profess knowledge: What do you know? But that is only another way of asking oneself the same question. I do not hear it asked very frequently these days.

Allen Tate

Princeton
January 16, 1941

ACKNOWLEDGMENTS

The author gratefully acknowledges his indebtedness to the following:

A Survey of Modernist Poetry, by Laura Riding and Robert Graves: Doubleday, Doran and Co.

They Say the Forties, by Howard Mumford Jones: Henry Holt and Co.

"Justice Denied in Massachusetts," from *The Buck in the Snow,* by Edna St. Vincent Millay (Harper and Brothers): by kind permission of Brandt and Brandt.

"Nature's Questioning," from *Collected Poems,* by Thomas Hardy: The Macmillan Co.

The Emperor Heart, by Laurence Whistler: The Macmillan Co.

Poems, by C. F. MacIntyre: The Macmillan Co.

English Pastoral Poetry, by William Empson: W. W. Norton and Co., 1926.

Science and Poetry, by I. A. Richards: W. W. Norton and Co.

Poetry and the Modern World, by David Daiches: The University of Chicago Press.

The Novel and the Modern World, by David Daiches: The University of Chicago Press.

xi

The Waste Land, by T. S. Eliot: Harcourt, Brace and Co.

Coleridge on the Imagination, by I. A. Richards: Harcourt, Brace and Co.

Poems, by W. H. Auden: Random House.

Darkling Plain, by Sara Bard Field: Random House.

The Philosophy of Rhetoric, by I. A. Richards: The Oxford University Press.

The Sleeping Fury, by Louise Bogan: Charles Scribner's Sons.

Monticello and Other Poems, by Lawrence Lee: Charles Scribner's Sons.

The World's Body, by John Crowe Ransom: Charles Scribner's Sons.

Selected Poems, by Allan Tate: Charles Scribner's Sons.

Jordan's Delight, by R. P. Blackmur: Arrow Editions.

Hardy of Wessex, by C. J. Weber: Columbia University Press.

Thomas Hardy, by William R. Rutland: Blackie and Sons.

Acknowledgment is also due the following magazines for material in this book previously published by them:

The Southern Review.

The New Republic.

The Virginia Quarterly Review.

The American Review.

The American Scholar.

CONTENTS

REASON IN MADNESS

CRITICAL ESSAYS

THE PRESENT FUNCTION
OF CRITICISM

Nous avons une impuissance de prouver, invincible à
tout le dogmatisme. Nous avons une idée de la vérité,
invincible à tout le pyrrhonisme.—PASCAL.

I

WE ARE not very much concerned when we confess
that communication among certain points of view
is all but impossible. Let us put three persons together
who soon discover that they do not agree. No matter; they
quickly find a procedure, a program, an objective. So they
do agree that there is something to be *done*, although they
may not be certain why they are doing it, and they may
not be interested in the results, the meaning of which is
not very important: before they can consider the meaning
they have started a new program. This state of mind is
positivism. It assumes that the communication of ideas
towards the formulation of truths is irrelevant to action;
the program is an end in itself. But if we are interested in
truth I believe that our intellectual confusion is such that
we can merely write that interest upon the record of our
time.

This essay represents a "point of view" which seems to
have little in common with other points of view that are
tolerated, and even applauded, today. It cannot be com-

municated at the level of the procedure and the program; it cannot, in short, be communicated to persons whose assumptions about life come out of positivism. (For positivism is not only a scientific movement; it is a moral attitude.) It has moved to contempt and rage persons whose intelligence I respect and admire.

The point of view here, then, is that historicism, scientism, psychologism, biologism, in general the confident use of the scientific vocabularies in the spiritual realm, has created or at any rate is the expression of a spiritual disorder. That disorder may be briefly described as a dilemma.

On the one hand, we assume that all experience can be ordered scientifically, an assumption that we are almost ready to confess has intensified if it has not actually created our distress; but on the other hand, this assumption has logically reduced the spiritual realm to irresponsible emotion, to what the positivists of our time see as irrelevant feeling; it is irrelevant because it cannot be reduced to the terms of positivist procedure. It is my contention here that the high forms of literature offer us the only complete, and thus the most reponsible, versions of our experience. The point of view of this essay, then, is influenced by the late, neglected T. E. Hulme (and not this essay alone). It is the belief, philosophically tenable, in a radical discontinuity between the physical and the spiritual realms.

In our time the historical approach to criticism, in so far as it has attempted to be a scientific method, has undermined the significance of the material which it proposes to investigate. On principle the sociological and historical scholar must not permit himself to see in the arts meanings that his method does not assume. To illustrate some of the wide implications of this method I will try to see it as more than a method: it is the temper of our age. It has profoundly influenced our politics and our education.

What will happen to literature under the totalitarian society that is coming in the next few years—it may be, so far as critical opinion is concerned, in the next few months? The question has got to be faced by literary critics, who as men of explicit ideas must to a great extent define for imaginative literature the *milieu* in which it will flourish or decay. The first ominous signs of this change are before us. The tradition of free ideas is as dead in the United States as it is in Germany. For at least a generation it has suffered a slow extinction, and it may receive the *coup de grâce* from the present war. The suppression of the critical spirit in this country will have sinister features that the official Nazi censorship, with all its ruthlessness, has not yet achieved, for the Nazis are, towards opinion, crude, objective, and responsible. Although it has only a harsh military responsibility, this censorship is definite, and it leaves the profession of letters in no doubt of its standing. Under this regime it has no standing at all. Increasingly since 1933 the critical intelligence under National Socialism has enjoyed the choice of extinction or frustration in exile.

Could the outlook be worse for the future of criticism?

In the United States we face the censorship of the pressure group. We have a tradition of irresponsible interpretation of patriotic necessity. We are entering a period in which we shall pay dearly for having turned our public education over to the professional "educationists" and the sociologists. These men have taught the present generation that the least thing about man is his intelligence, if he have it at all; the greatest thing his adjustment to Society (not to a good society): a mechanical society in which we were to be conditioned for the realization of a *bourgeois* paradise of gadgets and of the consumption, not of the fruits of the earth, but of commodities. Happily this degraded version of the myth of reason has been discredited by the course of what the liberal mind calls "world events"; and man will at any rate be spared the indignity of achieving it. What else can he now achieve? If history had dramatic form we might be able to see ourselves going down to destruction, with a small standard flying in the all but mindless hollow of our heads; and we should have our dignity to the end.

But this vision is too bright, too optimistic; for the "democracy" of appetites, drives, and stimulus-and-response has already affected us. What we thought was to be a conditioning process in favor of a state planned by Teachers College of Columbia University will be a conditioning equally useful for Plato's tyrant state. The actuality of tyranny we shall enthusiastically greet as the development of democracy, for the ringing of the democratic bell will make our political glands flow as freely for dictatorship, as, hitherto, for monopoly capitalism.

This hypocrisy is going to have a great deal to do with literary criticism because it is going to have a very definite effect upon American thought and feeling, at every level. There is no space here to track down the intellectual pedigree of the attitude of the social scientist. As early as 1911 Hilaire Belloc published a neglected book called *The Tyrant State,* in which he contended that the world revolution would not come out of the Second International. Nobody paid any attention to this prophecy; the Marxists ignored it for the obvious reason, and the liberals took it to mean that the world revolution would not happen at all. Belloc meant that the revolution was inherent in our pseudo-democratic intellectual tradition, buttressed by monopoly capitalism, and that the revolution would not proceed towards social justice, but would achieve the slave state. The point of view that I am sketching here looks upon the rise of the social sciences and their influence in education, from Comtism to Deweyism, as a powerful aid to the coming of the slave society. Under the myth of reason all the vast accumulation of *data* on social behavior, social control, social dynamics, was to have been used in building a pseudo-mystical and pseudo-democratic utopia on the Wellsian plan. In this vision of mindless perfection an elementary bit of historical insight was permitted to lapse: Plato had this insight, with less knowledge of history than we have. It is simply that, if you get a society made up of persons who have surrendered their humanity to the predatory impulses, the quickest way to improve matters is to call in a dictator; for when you lose the moral and religious authority, the military authority stands ready to supervene. Professor Dewey's social integration does not supervene. Under the actuality of history our sociological knowledge is a ready-made weapon that is now being used in Europe for the control of the people, and it will doubtless soon be used here for the same purpose.

To put this point of view into another perspective it is only necessary to remember that the intellectual movement variously known as positivism, pragmatism, instrumentalism, is the expression of a middle-class culture—a culture that we have achieved in America with so little consciousness of any other culture that we often say that a class description of it is beside the point. Matthew Arnold —in spite of his vacillating hopes for the middle class— said that one of its leading traits was lack of intelligence, and that industrialism, the creation of the middle class, had "materialized the upper class, vulgarized the middle class, and brutalized the lower class."

This lack of intelligence in our middle class, this vulgarity of the utilitarian attitude, is translatable into other levels of our intellectual activity. It is, for example, but a step from the crude sociologism of the normal school to the cloistered historical scholarship of the graduate school. We are all aware, of course, of the contempt in which the scholars hold the "educationists": yet the historical scholars, once the carriers of the humane tradition, have now merely the genteel tradition; the independence of judgment, the belief in intelligence, the confidence in literature, that informed the humane tradition, have disappeared; under the genteel tradition the scholars exhibit timidity of judgment, disbelief in intelligence, and suspicion of the value of literature. These attitudes of scholarship are the attitudes of the *haute bourgeoisie* that support it in the great universities; it is now commonplace to observe that the uncreative money-culture of modern times tolerates the historical routine of the scholars. The routine is "safe," and it shares with the predatory social process at large a naturalistic basis. And this naturalism easily bridges the thin gap between the teachers' college and the graduate school, between the sociologist and the literary source-hunter, between the comptometrist of literary "reactions" and the enumerator of influences.

The naturalism of the literary scholar is too obvious to need demonstration here; his substitution of "method" for intelligence takes its definite place in the positivistic movement which, from my point of view, has been clearing the way for the slave state; and the scholar must bear his part of the responsibility for the hypocrisy that will blind us to the reality of its existence, when it arrives.

The function of criticism should have been, in our time, as in all times, to maintain and to demonstrate the special, unique, and complete knowledge which the great forms of literature afford us. And I mean quite simply, *knowledge*, not historical documentation and information. But our literary critics have been obsessed by politics, and when they have been convinced of the social determinism of literature, they have been in principle indistinguishable from the academic scholars, who have demonstrated that literature does not exist, that it is merely history, which must be studied as history is studied, through certain scientific analogies. The scholars have not maintained the tradition of literature as a form of knowledge; by looking at it as merely one among many forms of social and political expression, they will have no defense against the censors of the power state, or against the hidden censors of the pressure group. Have the scholars not been saying all along that literature is only politics? Well, then, let's suppress it, since the politics of poets and novelists is notoriously unsound. And the scholars will say, yes, let's suppress it—our attempt to convert literature into science has done better than that: it has already extinguished it.

II

What the scholars are saying, of course, is that the meaning of a work of literature is identical with their method of studying it—a method that dissolves the literature into its history. Are the scholars studying literature, or are they not? That is the question. If they are not, why then do they continue to pretend that they are? This is the scholars' contribution to the intellectual hypocrisy of the positivistic movement. But when we come to the individual critics, the word hypocrisy will not do. When we think of the powerful semi-scientific method of studying poetry associated with the name of I. A. Richards, we may say that there is a certain ambiguity of critical focus.

Mr. Richards has been many different kinds of critic, one kind being an extremely valuable kind; but the role I have in mind here is that of *The Principles of Literary Criticism,* a curious and ingenious *tour de force* of a variety very common today. The species is: literature is not really nonsense, it is in a special way a kind of science; this particular variety is: poetry is a kind of applied psychology. I am not disposing of Mr. Richards in a sentence; like everybody else of my generation I have learned a great deal from him, even from what I consider his errors and evasions; and if it is these that interest me now, it is because they get more attention than his occasional and profound insights into the art of reading poetry.

In *The Principles of Literary Criticism* there is the significant hocus-pocus of impulses, stimuli, and responses; there are even the elaborate charts of nerves and nerve-systems that purport to show how the "stimuli" of poems elicit "responses" in such a way as to "organize our impulses" towards action; there is, throughout, the pretense that poetry is at last a laboratory science. How many innocent young men—myself among them—thought, in 1924, that laboratory jargon meant laboratory demonstration! But for a certain uneasiness evinced by Mr. Richards in the later chapters, one could fairly see this book as a typical instance of the elaborate cheat that the positivistic movement has perpetrated upon the human spirit. For the uneasy conscience of one Richards, a thousand critics and scholars have not hesitated to write literary history, literary biography, literary criticism, with facile confidence in whatever scientific analogies came to hand.

With the candor of a generous spirit Mr. Richards has repudiated his early scientism: the critical conscience that struggled in the early work against the limitations of a positivist education won out in the end. What did Mr. Richards give up? It is not necessary to be technical about it. He had found that the picture of the world passed on to us by the poetry of the pre-scientific ages was scientifically false. The *things* and *processes* pointed to by the poets, even the modern poets, since they too were backward in the sciences, could not be verified by any of the known scientific procedures. As a good positivist he saw the words of a poem as *referents,* and referents have got to refer to something—which the words of even the best poem failed to do. If Mr. Richards could have read Carnap and Morris in the early twenties, he would have said that poems may *designate* but they do not *denote,* because you can designate something that does not exist, like a purple cow. Poems designate things that do not exist, and are compacted of *pseudo-statements,* Mr. Richards's most famous invention in scientese; that is, false statements, or just plain lies.

Perhaps the best way to describe Mr. Richards's uneasiness is to say that, a year or two later, in his pamphlet-size book, *Science and Poetry,* he came up short against Matthew Arnold's belief that the future of poetry was immense, that, religion being gone, poetry would have to take its place. The curious interest of Arnold's argument cannot detain us. It is enough to remember that even in *The Principles of Literary Criticism* Mr. Richards was coming round to that view. Not that poetry would bring back religion, or become a new religion! It would perform the therapeutic offices of religion, the only part of it worth keeping. In short, poetry would "order" our minds; for although science was true, it had failed to bring intellectual order—it had even broken up the older order of pseudo-statement; and although poetry was false, it would order our minds, whatever this ordering might mean.

To order our minds with lies became, for a few years, Mr. Richards's program, until at last, in *Coleridge on the Imagination* (1935), the Sisyphean effort to translate Coleridge into naturalistic terms broke down; and now, I believe, Mr. Richards takes the view that poetry, far from being a desperate remedy, is an independent form of knowledge, a kind of cognition, equal to the knowledge of the sciences at least, perhaps superior. The terms in which Mr. Richards frames this insight need not concern us here: [1] I have sketched his progress towards it in order to remind you that the repudiation of a literal positivism by its leading representative in modern criticism has not been imitated by his followers, or by other critics who, on a different road, have reached Mr. Richards's position of ten years ago. They are still there. Whether they are sociologists in criticism or practitioners of the routine of historical "correlation," they alike subscribe to a single critical doctrine. It is the Doctrine of Relevance.

[1] See p. 52 ff. for a more detailed discussion of this point.

III

The Doctrine of Relevance is very simple. It means that the subject-matter of a literary work must not be isolated in terms of form; it must be tested (on an analogy to scientific techniques) by observation of the world that it "represents." Are the scene, the action, the relations of the characters in a novel, in some verifiable sense true? It is an old question. It has given rise in our time to various related sorts of criticism that frequently produce great insights. (I think here of Mr. Edmund Wilson's naturalistic interpretation of James's *The Turn of the Screw*. Mr. Wilson's view is not the whole view, but we can readily see that we had been missing the whole view until he added his partial view.)

The criterion of relevance, as we saw with Mr. Richards, has a hard time of it with an art like poetry. Of all the arts, poetry has a medium the most complex and the least reducible to any one set of correlations, be they historical, or economic, or theological, or moral. From the point of view of direct denotation of objects about all that we can say about one of Keats's odes is what I heard a child say— "It is something about a bird."

But with the novel the case is different, because the novel is very close to history—indeed, in all but the great novelists, it is not clearly set off from history. I do not intend here to get into Aristotle and to argue the difference between history and fiction. It is plain that action and character, to say nothing of place and time, point with less equivocation to observed or perhaps easily observable phenomena than even the simplest poetry ever does. The novel points with some directness towards history—or I might say with Mr. David Daiches, to the historical process.

I mention Mr. Daiches because his *The Novel and the Modern World* seems to me to be one of the few good books on contemporary fiction. Yet at bottom it is an example of what I call the Doctrine of Relevance, and I believe that he gains every advantage implicit in that doctrine, and suffers, in the range and acuteness of his perceptions, probably none of its limitations. I cannot do justice to Mr. Daiches's treatment of some of the best novelists of our time; my quotations from his final essay—which is a summary view of his critical position—will do him less than justice. His statement of his method seems to me to be narrower than his critical practice:

The critic who endeavors to see literature as a process rather than as a series of phenomena, and as a process which is bound up with an infinite series of ever wider processes, ought to realize that however wide his context, it is but a fraction of what it might be.

Admirable advice; but what concerns me in this passage is the assumption that Mr. Daiches shares with the historical scholar, that literature is to be understood chiefly as a part of the historical process. He goes on to say:

The main object is to indicate relevance and to show how understanding depends on awareness of relevance. That appreciation depends on understanding and that a theory of value can come only after appreciation, hardly need noting.

I must confess that after a brilliant performance of two hundred ten pages I feel that Mr. Daiches has let us down a little here. I am aware that he enters a shrewd list of warnings and exceptions, but I am a little disappointed to learn that he sees himself as applying to the novel a criterion of historical relevance not very different from the criterion of the graduate school. It is likely that I misunderstand Mr. Daiches. He continues:

> The patterning of those events [in a novel], their relation to each other within the story, the attitude to them which emerges, the mood which surrounds them, the tone in which they are related, and the style of the writing are all equally relevant.

Yes: but relevant to what? And are they *equally* relevant? The equality of relevance points to historical documentation; or may we assume here that since the "main object is to indicate relevance," the critic must try to discover the relevance of history to the work? Or the work to history? What Mr. Daiches seems to me to be saying is that the function of criticism is to bring the work back to history, and to test its relevance to an ascertainable historical process. Does relevance then mean some kind of identity with an historical process? And since "understanding depends on awareness of relevance," is it understanding of history or of the novel; or is it of both at once? That I am not wholly wrong in my grasp of the terms relevance and process is borne out by this passage:

He [the critic] can neither start with a complete view of civilization and work down to the individual work of art, nor can he start with the particular work of art and work up to civilization as a whole; he must try both methods and give neither his complete trust.

Admirable advice again; but are there actually two methods here? Are they not both the historical method? When Mr. Daiches says that it is possible to start from the individual work of art and work *up* (interesting adverb, as interesting as the *down* to which you go in order to reach the work of art), he doubtless alludes to what he and many other critics today call the "formalist" method. Mr. Daiches nicely balances the claims of formalist and historian. The formalist is the critic who doesn't work up, but remains where he started, with the work of art—the "work in itself," as Mr. Daiches calls it, "an end which, though attainable, is yet unreal." Its unreality presumably consists in the critic's failure to be aware of the work's relevance to history. There may have been critics like Mr. Daiches's formalist monster, but I have never seen one, and I doubt that Mr. Daiches himself, on second thought, would believe he exists. (Or perhaps he was Aristotle, who said that the nature of tragedy is in its structure, not its reception by the audience.) I am not sure. As a critic of the novel Mr. Daiches is acutely aware

of unhistorical meanings in literature, but as a critical
theorist he seems to me to be beating his wings in the
unilluminated tradition of positivism. That tradition has
put the stigma of "formalism" upon the unhistorical meaning. Critics of our age nervously throw the balance in favor
of the historical lump. Mr. Daiches's plea for it rests upon
its superior inclusiveness; the historical scholar can make
formal analyses against the background of history; he has
it both ways, while the formalist has it only one, and that
one "unreal." But here, again, Mr. Daiches's insight into
the vast complexity of the critic's task prompts at least a
rueful misgiving about the "wider context"; he admits the
superiority of the historian, "though it may be replied that
inclusiveness is no necessary proof of such superiority." At
this point Mr. Daiches becomes a little confused.

I have the strong suspicion in reading Mr. Daiches (I
have it in reading the late Marxists and the sociological
and historical scholars) that critics of the positivist school
would not study literature at all if it were not so handy
in libraries; they don't really like it; or they are at any
rate ashamed of it—because it is "unreal." The men of our
time who have the boldness and the logical rigor to stand
by the implications of their position are the new logical
positivists at Chicago—Carnap and Morris, whom I have already mentioned; they are quite firm in their belief—with
a little backsliding on the part of Morris [2]—that poetry,

---

[2] Charles W. Morris, "Science, Art, and Technology," in *The Kenyon
Review*, Autumn 1939. Mr. Morris argues that, although poetry is non-
sense semantically, it is the realm of "value."

and perhaps all imaginative literature, is, in Mr. Arthur Mizener's phrase, only "amiable insanity": it designates but it does not denote anything "real."

I respect this attitude because it is barbarism unabashed and unashamed. But of the positivists who still hanker after literature with yearnings that come out of the humane tradition, what can be said? The ambiguity—or since we are in our mental climate and no longer with persons—the hypocrisy of our liberal intellectual tradition appears again; or let us say the confusion. Is Mr. Daiches wrestling with a critical theory, or is he only oscillating between the extremes of a dilemma? From the strict, logical point of view he is entitled merely to the positivist horn, as the general critical outlook of our age is so entitled.

This ought to be the end of literature, if literature were logical; it is not logical but tough; and after the dark ages of our present enlightenment it will flourish again. This essay has been written from a point of view which does not admit the validity of the rival claims of formalism and history, of art-for-art's-sake and society. Literature is the complete knowledge of man's experience, and by knowledge I mean that unique and formed intelligence of the world of which man alone is capable.

LITERATURE AS KNOWLEDGE
Comment and Comparison

MATTHEW ARNOLD'S war on the Philistines was fought, as everybody knows; but nobody thinks that it was won. Arnold conducted it in what he considered to be the scientific spirit. The Philistines had a passion for "acting and instituting," but they did not know "what we ought to act and to institute." This sort of knowledge must be founded upon "the scientific passion for knowing." But it must not stop there. Culture, which is the study of perfection and the constant effort to achieve it, is superior to the scientific spirit because it includes and passes beyond it. Arnold was, in short, looking for a principle of unity, but it must be a unity of experience. There was before him the accumulating body of the inert, descriptive facts of science, and something had to be done about it.

Yet if it is true, as T. S. Eliot said many years ago, that were Arnold to come back he would have his work to do all over again, he would at any rate have to do it very differently. His program, culture added to science and perhaps correcting it, has been our program for nearly a century, and it has not worked. For the facts of science are not inert facts waiting for the poet, as emblematic guardian

of culture, to bring to life in the nicely co-operative enterprise of scientist and poet which the nineteenth century
put its faith in. In this view the poet is merely the scientist
who achieves completeness. "It is a result of no little culture," Arnold says, "to attain to a clear perception that
science and religion are two wholly different things." Religion had yielded to the "fact" of science, but poetry on
a positive scientific base could take over the work of religion, and its future was "immense." The "fact" had
undermined religion, but it could support poetry.

Although Arnold betrayed not a little uneasiness about
this easy solution, it was his way of putting literature upon
an equal footing with science. If Arnold failed, can we
hope to succeed? Whether literature and science considered philosophically, as Coleridge would phrase it, are the
same thing, or different but equal, or the one subordinate
to the other, has become a private question. It does not
concern the public at large. While Arnold's poet was ex-
tending the hand of fellowship to the scientist, the scientist
did not return the greeting; for never for an instant did
he see himself as the inert and useful partner in an enterprise of which he would not be permitted to define the
entire scope. He was not, alas, confined to the inertia of
fact; his procedure was dynamic all along; and it was ani-
mated by the confident spirit of positivism which has captured the modern world.

Had he been what Arnold thought he was, how conveniently the partnership would have worked! For what
was Arnold's scientist doing? He was giving us exact ob-

servation and description of the external world. The poet
could give us that, and he could add to it exact observation and description of man's inner life, a realm that the
positivist would never be so bold as to invade. But the poet's
advantage was actually twofold. Not only did he have this
inner field of experience denied to the scientist, he had a
resource which was his peculiar and hereditary right—
figurative language and the power of rhetoric.

If the inert fact alone could not move us, poetic diction
could make it moving by heightening it; for poetry is
"thought and art in one." This is an injustice to Arnold;
he was a great critic of ideas, of currents of ideas, of the
situation of the writer in his time; and from this point
of view his theory of poetry is of secondary importance.
But since I am now interested in the failure, ours as well
as his, to understand the relation of poetry and science, it
has been necessary to put his poetic theory in terms that
will bring out its defects. On one side it is an eighteenth-
century view of poetic language as the rhetorical vehicle
of ideas; and it is connected with Arnold's famous definition of religion as "morality touched with emotion."
Poetry is descriptive science or experience at that level,
touched with emotion.

If Arnold had taste, he had very simple analytical
powers, and we are never quite convinced by his fine quotations from the poets. Why is this so? Because he admires
good things for bad reasons; or because at any rate his
reasons invariably beg the question. In the famous passage
on Dryden and Pope in "The Study of Poetry" these poets

are not poetic because they are not *poetic*. (Arnold himself is responsible for the italics.) And he looks to us for immediate assent to a distinction between a "prose" classic and a "poetic" classic that has not been actually made. He cites his "touchstones" for the purpose of moving us, and the nice discrimination of feeling which awareness of the touchstones induces will permit us to judge other passages of verse in terms of feeling. The "high seriousness" is partly the elevated tone, a tone which is a quality of the poet's feeling about his subject: it is the poet's business to communicate it to the reader.

This attitude, this tone, centers in emotion. But its relation to what it is about, whether it is external to the subject or inherent in it, Arnold refuses to make clear. The high seriousness may be said to reflect the subject, which must have Aristotelian magnitude and completeness. Arnold had a shrewd sense of the disproportions of tone and subject which he developed into a principle in the Preface to the 1853 edition of his poems. He was suppressing the very fine "Empedocles on Aetna" because, he said, it has no action; it is all passive suffering; and passive suffering is not a proper subject for poetry. (A view that has been revived in our time by the late W. B. Yeats.) Action, then, is the subject of the greatest poetry. This conviction is so strong—who will question its rightness, *as far as it goes?*—that he actually puts into quotation marks words which are not quoted from anybody at all but which represent for him the consensus of the ancients on the importance of action: " 'All depends upon the subject; choose a fitting action, penetrate yourself with the feeling of its situations; this done, everything else will follow.'" But will everything else follow? Does a great style follow? To a gift for action Shakespeare "added a special one of his own; a gift, namely, of happy, abundant, and ingenious expression...." I think we should attend closely here to the words "added" and "ingenious," for they reveal Arnold's view of the function of language. And suppose you have lyric poetry which may be, like Arnold's own fine lyrics, more meditative than dramatic, and more concerned with the futility of action than with action itself? It has never, I believe, been pointed out that the Preface of 1853 cuts all the props from under lyric poetry. The lyric at its best is "dramatic," but there is no evidence that Arnold thought it so; for the lyric, though it may be a moment of action, lacks magnitude and completeness; it may be the beginning, or the middle, or the end, but never all three. What, then, is the subject of the lyric? Is it all feeling, nothing but feeling? It is feeling about "ideas," not actions; and the feeling communicates "power and joy."

This gross summary of Arnold's poetics omits all the sensitive discriminations that he felt in reading the poets; it omits all but the framework of his thought. Yet the framework alone must concern us on this occasion. Arnold is still the great critical influence in the universities, and it is perhaps not an exaggeration of his influence to say that debased Arnold is the main stream of popular appreciation of poetry. It would be fairer to say that Arnold the critic was superior to his critical theory; yet at the distance of three generations we may look back upon his lack of a critical dialectic—he even had a certain contempt for it in other critics—as a calamity for that culture which it was his great desire to strengthen and pass on.

His critical theory was elementary, and if you compare him with Coleridge a generation earlier, he represents a loss. His position is nearer to the neo-classicism of Lessing, whom he praises in *Culture and Anarchy* for humanizing knowledge, a leveling-off of distinctions of which Lessing as a matter of fact was not guilty. He shares with Lessing the belief—but not its dialectical basis—that the language of poetry is of secondary importance to the subject, that it is less difficult than the medium of painting, and that, given the action, all else follows.

This remnant of neo-classicism in Arnold has been ably discerned by Mr. Cleanth Brooks in *Modern Poetry and the Tradition*. I go into it here not to deny that action is necessary to the long poem; for Arnold's view contains a fundamental truth. But it is not the whole truth; asserted in his terms, it may not be a truth at all. The important question goes further. It is: What is the relation of language to the "subject," to the dramatic and narrative subject as action, or to the lyrical subject as "idea"? The question may be pushed even further: Is it possible finally to distinguish the language from the subject? Are not subject and language one?

For Arnold the subject is what we commonly call the prose subject; that is to say, as much of the poetic subject as we can put into ordinary prose. The poet takes it up at the level at which the scientist—or Arnold's simulacrum of him—takes it: the level of observation and description. The poet now puts it into language that will bring the inert facts to life and move us. The language is strictly what Mr. Richards calls the "vehicle"—it does not embody the subject; it conveys it and remains external to it.

For what are action and subject? The positivists have their own notion of these terms; and their language of physical determinism suits that notion better than the poet's. The poet's language is useless.

II

Is it not easy to see how such a poetics gives the case for poetry away to the scientist? Not to Arnold's straw scientist, who politely kept to his descriptive place and left to literature man's evaluation of his experience; but to the scientist as he is: a remarkably ingenious and dynamic fellow whose simple fanaticism brooks no compromise with his special projects. Whatever these on occasion may be, he demands an exact one-to-one relevance of language to the objects and the events to which it refers. In this relevance lies the "meaning" of all terms and propositions in so far as they are used for the purpose of giving us valid knowledge. It is, of course, knowledge for action; and apart from this specific purpose, the problem of meaning is not even a real problem.

"Meaning" has been replaced by a concept of "operational validity"—that is to say, the "true" meaning of a term is not its definition; it is the number of statements containing it which can be referred to empirically observed events. Along with meaning and definition, universals also disappear; and with universals, cognition. A proposition does not represent an act of knowing by a knower—that is, a mind; it is, in a chemical metaphor, the expression of an interaction among certain elements of a "situation."

This advanced position in the philosophy of science has been set forth in the new *International Encyclopedia of Unified Science,* which is being published serially at the University of Chicago. Of great interest from the point of view of literary criticism are the brilliant studies of "semiosis," or the functioning of language as "signs." Mr. Charles W. Morris's "Foundations for the Theory of Signs," [1] is a model of exact exposition in a field of enormous complication. This field is popularly known as "semantics," but semantics in any exact sense is only one "dimension" of semiosis. In this brief glance at the aesthetic and critical implications of Mr. Morris's writings, his theory as a whole cannot be set forth.

Semiosis is the actual functioning of language in three dimensions which are located and described by means of the science of "semiotic." Semiotic, then, is the study of semiosis. The three dimensions in which all language, verbal, or mathematical, functions are: (1) the semantical, (2) the syntactical, and (3) the pragmatical; and the respective studies in these dimensions are semantics, syn-

[1] *International Encyclopedia of Unified Science,* Vol. I, No. 2.

tactics, and pragmatics. It must be borne in mind that in semiosis the three dimensions are never separate; in semiotic they are distinguished abstractly for study. Semiotic looks towards the formation of rules which will govern the use of all language (signs), and it lays claim to an ultimate unification of all "knowledge."

That need not concern us here. Let us take a simple declarative sentence: "This county has an annual rainfall of fifty-one inches." From the semantical point of view the sentence designates certain conditions, or a situation: it is the "sign-vehicle" for that designation. If upon investigation we find that the situation actually exists, then it has not only been designated; it has also been *denoted*. From the syntactical point of view we are not concerned with what the sign-vehicle points to; for syntactics deals with the formal structure of the sentence, the relations of the words. From the pragmatical point of view the meaning of the sentence is the effect it has upon somebody who hears it or reads it. If I am about to buy a farm in this county, and learn that "this county has an annual rainfall of fifty-one inches," I may go elsewhere; at the moment I hear the sentence I may light a cigarette, or look the other way; or laugh or swear. All this behavior would be the functioning of the sign in the pragmatic dimension.

The complex possibilities of semiotic may not be evident in this crude summary. Mr. Morris says: "The sign vehicle itself is simply one object." It is an object that may function in other sign-vehicles; it may be designated, denoted, or reacted to; and the process is infinite. The identification of signs and their relations is equally complex. There are, for example, a characterizing sign, a symbolic sign, an indexical sign, and an iconic sign; and any of these, in certain contexts, may function as any other. I shall return to them presently.

The only philosophic criticism of this system that I have seen is Howard D. Roelofs' article in the symposium on the "New Encyclopedists," published in the *Kenyon Review* (Spring 1939). Mr. Roelofs is concerned with Mr. Morris's rejection of the problem of universals and of cognition. It ought to be plain from my brief exposition of the pragmatic dimension of semiosis that the significant factor is what I *do*, not what I *think*, leading to what I do; and that thus the bias of the science of semiotic is pragmatic in the ordinary sense, and even behavioristic. For Mr. Morris says: "A 'concept' [i.e., a universal] may be regarded as a semantical rule determining the use of characterizing signs." Mr. Roelofs' comment is interesting:

Morris has no trouble with this problem [i.e., the problem of universals]. It is simply a rule of our language that such a term as "man" can be used as often as the conditions stated in its definition are fulfilled. That makes the term a universal. If we then ask how it happens those conditions are in fact frequently fulfilled, we are informed, "It can only be said the world is such." And those who are tempted by this fact to believe that universals are somehow objective, functioning in nature, are silenced with a threat: to talk as if universals were entities in the world is "to utter pseudo-thing sentences of the quasi-semantical type."... the heart of the problem is

dismissed with a phrase and a language rule offered as a
solution.

The bearing of Mr. Roelofs' criticism will be plainer in a
moment. Now Mr. Morris, in discussing the syntactical
dimension, says: "Syntactics, as the study of the syntactical
relations of signs to one another *in abstraction* from the
relations of signs to objects or to interpreters [persons], is
the best developed of all the branches of semiotic." Exactly; because syntactics comes out of traditional formal
logic and grammar, and because it "deliberately neglects
what has here been called the semantical and the pragmatical dimensions of semiosis."

The role of syntactics in the semiotic science remains
somewhat obscure; it seems to consist in a number of
"transformation rules"—that is, in formulas by which given
expressions in words, numbers, or symbols can be changed
into equivalent but formally different expressions. What
power of the mind there may be which enables us in the
first place to form these expressions nowhere appears. (I
daresay this statement is of the quasi-semantical type.) But
Mr. Morris tells us how we are to think of the rules of the
three dimensions of semiotic:

Syntactical rules determine the sign relations between sign
vehicles; semantical rules correlate sign vehicles with other
objects; pragmatical rules state the conditions in the interpreters under which the sign vehicle is a sign. Any rule when
actually in use operates as a type of behavior, and in this
sense there is a pragmatical component in all rules.

If we imagine with Mr. Roelofs a situation in which semiosis is functioning, we shall see pretty clearly the behavioristic tendency of the science of semiotic; and we shall also see in what sense "there is a pragmatical component in all rules." A simplified process of semiosis, or the actual functioning of signs, is very easy to state. There is first of all the sign, which we get in terms of a sign-vehicle. It looks two ways; first, it points to something, designates something; and, secondly, what is designated elicits a response from persons who are present. The thing pointed to is thus the *designatum;* the response is the *interpretant.* By implication there is an interpreter, a person, a mind; but Mr. Morris is consistently vague about him: he is not a technical factor, he is a superfluous entity, in semiosis. That is to say, not only is he not needed in order to explain the functioning of signs; he would embarrass the explanation. Mr. Roelofs makes this clear, as follows:

The innocent reader will take the analysis of the use of signs to be the analysis of a cognitive process. The correctness of the analysis as far as it goes conceals the fact that cognition itself has been eliminated. Consider this illustration. A maid enters the room and says to the three persons present, "The doctor called." One person thereupon takes a pen and writes a line in a diary; the second goes to a telephone and makes a call; the third says, "Did he?" According to the analysis offered by Morris, the words uttered by the maid are the sign-vehicle. The actual call of the doctor is the denotatum.[2]

---

[2] *Denotata* are real things; *designata* may be pointed to, but they are not necessarily real. For example, the Phoenix' "spicy nest." The doctor's call is a *designatum* which is also a *denotatum*—it's "real."

The three persons are the interpreters, and their three different actions are the interpretants, the responses of the interpreters to the denotatum via the sign-vehicle. No one is likely to deny these factors are present. It should be noted that the interpretants, to the extent that they are a sequence of physical actions, can be perceived. It should also be noted that such sequences of action are not cognitions... they are "interpretants," but their being such depends upon the cognitions of the interpreters. These responses are not themselves knowledge. They do depend upon knowledge, and that is precisely what Morris leaves out.... Morris objects to the term "meaning." This is not surprising. His analysis leaves out meaning in the primary sense of meaning. This is not to say that meanings are "like marbles" [Morris's phrase]. Meanings, indeed, like knowledge in general, are a unique kind of thing. There is literally nothing like knowledge except knowledge itself.

I have quoted Mr. Roelofs at length because what he has to say about the problem of cognition bears directly upon the semiotic version of the aesthetic problem. He sums up his argument:

The procedure culminates in eliminating not only universals, but cognition itself. Just as the answer to the problem of universals is that they do not exist [that is, they are only a semantical rule], the answer to the problem of knowledge is that there is no such thing. There are responses, but no cognition; there is a language, but not knowledge. Knowledge cannot be reduced to exclusively perceptual terms. Therefore

it does not exist. This is not empiricism. *It is positivism.*
[Italics mine.]

In this positivist technique for the analysis of language,
the interpreting mind, the cognizing intelligence, is lost
in the perceptual account of its external behavior. Mr.
Morris says: "In general, from the point of view of behavior, signs are 'true' in so far as they correctly determine
the expectations of the users, and so release more fully
the behavior which is implicitly aroused in the expecta-
tion or interpretation."

In Mr. Morris's aesthetics there is an aesthetic sign. Does
it implicitly—or explicitly—arouse expectations in terms of
behavior? Does it correctly determine our expectations?
Is the aesthetic sign "true" in that it is a determinant of
our behavior? Mr. Morris is not unequivocal in his answers
to these questions.

III

No—and yes, replies Mr. Morris, in two essays [3] the cun-
ning and scholastic ingenuity of which make even the
beautiful essay on the general theory of signs look ama-
teurish. No, he says, because the aesthetic sign is a special
sort of sign: it is *iconic*. It does not correctly determine
our behavior. Yes, because it bears the formidable responsibility of showing us what we ought to try to get out of

[3] "Esthetics and the Theory of Signs," in *The Journal of Unified Science,*
VIII, 1-3, pp. 131-150; and "Science, Art, and Technology," *The Kenyon
Review,* I, 4, pp. 409-423.

our behavior. The function of the aesthetic sign is nothing less than the "vivid presentation" of *values,* a presentation that is not only vivid, but *immediate*—without mediation —for direct apprehension. The iconic sign, in other words, designates without denoting; or if it does denote anything its *denotatum* is already in its own "properties." "In certain kinds of insanity," writes Mr. Morris, "the distinction between the designatum and the denotatum vanishes; the troublesome world of existences is pushed aside, and the frustrated *interests* [italics mine] get what satisfaction they can in the domain of signs...." Likewise *designata* and *denotata* become in aesthetics the same thing; but in this logical shuffle, worthy of a thirteenth-century *doctor subtilis,* the aesthetic sign is never confused "with the object it designates." It is that alone which saves it from the ignominy of insanity.

The difficulties of this theory must already be apparent. First, the difference between insanity and art is the hair's-breadth line, in the interpreter's response to the sign, between substituting the sign for reality and maintaining the distinction between sign and reality. The first question that one must ask, then, is this: With what does the interpreter make this distinction? If the distinction is not inherent in the nature of the sign, does the interpreter not perform an act of cognition? If the distinction is a mere interpretant, a behavioristic response, why do we not respond to a work of art uniformly; and why is that uniform response in every case not insane *unless we are capa-*

ble of a primary act of knowledge, of simply knowing the difference?

Secondly, if art is the realm of values—that is, if the peculiar nature of the aesthetic sign is that it shall convey values—the values must be inherent in the aesthetic sign, and must therefore compel in the interpreter the distinction between value and insanity; so that there is no possibility that the interpreter, who is incapable of cognition, will confuse the mere sign with reality. For the nature of the sign must determine the interpretant, or response.

There must therefore be a special "differentia" for the aesthetic sign that distinguishes it from all other signs whatever. "Lyric poetry," Mr. Morris says, "has a syntax and uses terms which designate things, but the syntax and the terms are so used that what stand out for the reader are values and evaluations." [4] Does not Mr. Morris confess his difficulty when he uses the vague metaphorical expression, "stand out," and the even more vague "so used"? Just what is this use? It is significant that in Mr. Morris's two articles on aesthetics, in which the word poetry frequently appears, there is no actual analysis of a passage or even of a line of verse; and not even a quotation from any poem in any language. He contents himself with assertions that the future of semiotic in the field of poetry is immense, and that only the work has to be done.

Now, if the contradiction that I have pointed out in general terms exists, we may see its origin if we examine further Mr. Morris's idea of the aesthetic sign. It is a

[4] "Foundations for the Theory of Signs," p. 58.

special variety of the iconic sign. To illustrate this it will be sufficient to relate the iconic to the characterizing sign, and to distinguish the icon from the symbol.

A characterizing sign [he says], characterizes that which it can denote. Such a sign may do this by exhibiting in itself the properties an object must have to be denoted by it, and in this case the characterizing sign is an *icon;* if this is not so, the characterizing sign may be called a *symbol.* A photograph, a star chart, a model, a chemical diagram, are icons, while the word "photograph," the names of the stars and of chemical elements are symbols.

The terminology is quite special. Icon is the Greek (εἰκών) for a sculptured figure. Ordinarily a symbol is what Mr. Morris claims for the icon: it exhibits in itself the qualities it stands for—like Christ on the Cross; or it represents by convention something other than itself, like πr^2 for the circumference of a circle. But here the terms are roughly equivalent, icon to image, symbol to concept; but only roughly, since in Mr. Morris's list of symbols "photograph" is not any particular photograph, while the name of a star must be the name of a particular star. There is a fundamental obscurity, that we shall have to pass over, in attributing to verbal language a thoroughly *iconic* property. In the list of icons, there are *a* photograph, *a* star chart, *a* model, *a* chemical diagram—all of them spatial and perceptual objects; but, while language is always used in a spatial setting, words appear in temporal sequence, and have only the spatial character of their occasion. We cannot *see* the properties of words in the words. We have simply got to know *what* the words convey. The phrase "a star chart" is not a star chart itself. Mr. Morris appears to have found in the term *icon,* at any rate so far as it pertains to aesthetics, merely a convenient evasion of the term *image;* for image would doubtless have held him in the old ontological aesthetics.

The essay, "Esthetics and the Theory of Signs," deals with the specific problem "of stating the differentia of the esthetic sign." Mr. Morris is constantly reminding us that iconic signs appear in all discourse, and that all discourse is by no means aesthetic discourse. Yet the special function of the iconic sign makes it possible for us to use it as the aesthetic sign; and that function is stated in a "semantical rule":

The semantical rule for the use of an iconic sign is that it denotes any object which has the properties (in practice, a selection from the properties) which it itself has. Hence when an interpreter apprehends an iconic sign-vehicle he apprehends directly what is designated; here mediated and unmediated taking account of certain properties both occur; [5] put in still other terms, every iconic sign has its own sign-vehicle among its denotata.

This is a difficult conception; perhaps it can be illustrated with a few lines of verse:

> *That time of year thou mayst in me behold*
> *When yellow leaves, or none, or few do hang*
> *Upon those boughs which shake against the cold . . .*

[5] There seems to be evidence in this clause that Mr. Morris is not interested in syntactics.

According to Mr. Morris, the sign-vehicle here would be the leaves hanging on the boughs. This verbal sign-vehicle has the "properties" of the natural objects which it designates; and that which it denotes is in the designation itself. That is, leaves-bough does not point to a definite situation or condition beyond itself: we get "directly what is designated" because it is of the nature of the iconic sign to contain its own *denotatum*. (I have simplified this analysis by ignoring "That time of year," which I believe would make it impossible to apply Mr. Morris's terms coherently.)

The treatment of the iconic sign in semiotic is mysterious. If any generalization about it is legitimate, we may surmise that certain terms, which Mr. Morris calls "primary terms," are untranslatable; that is to say, they cannot be handled by any principle of reduction; they have a certain completeness and finality. They denote themselves; certain iconic signs seem to be such terms. They are sign-vehicles for images, and our apprehension of them is direct. For while the iconic sign may denote something beyond itself, its specific character as an iconic sign is that part of what it denotes is the sign itself. "These facts," says Mr. Morris, "taken alone, do not delimit the esthetic sign, for blueprints, photographs, and scientific models are all iconic signs—but seldom works of art." He continues in a passage of great interest:

If, however, the designatum of an iconic sign be a *value* [italics mine] (and of course not all iconic signs designate values), the situation is changed: there is now not merely the designation of value properties (for such designation takes place even in science), nor merely the functioning of iconic signs (for these as such need not be esthetic signs), but there is the direct apprehension of value properties through the very presence of that which itself has the value it designates.

There are thus three steps in the "delimitation" of the aesthetic sign: First, it is an iconic sign; secondly, it is an iconic sign which designates a value; thirdly, it is an iconic sign which designates a value in the sign itself, so that our "apprehension" of that value is unmediated, that is, *direct*.

The difficulties created by this aesthetic doctrine are slippery and ambiguous. We may, for convenience, see them in two ways. The first set of problems lies in the term "apprehension"; the second, in the term "value."

The primary meaning of apprehension is a grasping or a taking hold of. What does Mr. Morris mean? If it means taking hold of by means of perception, we are asked to see ourselves *perceiving a value;* but a value cannot be an object of perception. If, however, apprehension means a direct, unmediated knowledge of a value, then there is an act of evaluation involved which implies the presence of a knowing mind. For the implied "semantical rule" for the aesthetic sign obviously forbids us to check the value wholly in terms of a situation external to the properties of the sign itself. We have got to *know* the value in itself; and only in an act of cognition can we know it. But if Mr. Morris means by apprehension the response, or mere "interpretant," of semiosis, it is a difficult thing to see how a mere response can be semantically correct unless the sign-vehicle points to a situation outside itself in terms of which the response is relevant. If there is no such situation, is not the interpretant a piece of insanity?

I cannot see how there can be any direct apprehension unless there is an agency to do the apprehending; and the interpretant is not an agent, it is a response. "One additional point may be noted to confirm the sign status of the work of art: The artist often draws attention to the sign-vehicle in such a way as to prevent the interpreter from merely reacting to it as an object and not as a sign...." Mr. Morris's phrases, "in such a way," "so used that," remain painfully evasive. What is that way? Now, if the preventive factor is inherent in the work of art, why did not the birds refrain from trying to eat the grapes in Zeuxis's picture? The citizens of Athens did not mistake the sign-vehicle for an object. Why? Because they *knew* the difference.

Mr. Morris's theory of value will further illuminate his difficulty. It is an "interest" theory of value for which he acknowledges an indebtedness to the pragmatic tradition of Mead and Dewey. Objects, according to this ancient theory, have value in relation to interests. "Values," says Mr. Morris, "are consummatory properties of objects or situations which answer to the consummation of interested acts." If I satisfy my hunger by eating a banana, the banana has value in relation to the specific interest, hunger. Does it follow that we have similar aesthetic interests, which we satisfy similarly? No specific aesthetic interest appears in semiosis. The aesthetic satisfaction proceeds from the frustration of "real" interests, from the blockage of interests as they drive onward to real "consummations." The aesthetic sign is a value that has not been consummated. Art is the expression of what men desire but are not getting.

There are two passages in "Esthetics and the Theory of Signs" which reveal the fundamental ambiguity in Mr. Morris's conception of the aesthetic sign as a "value." We shall be struck, I believe, by the remarkable parallel between Mr. Morris's view of the aesthetic medium and the neo-classical view, which we saw in Matthew Arnold.

Even though the complexity of the total icon is so very great that no denotatum (other than the esthetic sign vehicle itself) can in actuality be found, the work of art can still be considered a sign—for there can be designation without denotation.

But can the aesthetic sign—and this is the center of the problem—designate an interest "value" if it does not point to an interest? It seems to me that it cannot be a value in any "interest" theory of value whatever. And when the aesthetic sign is so complex that it does not lead to denotation, is not this complexity a semantical failure so great that Mr. Morris actually ought to take it to an institution for the insane?

The traditional prestige of the arts is formidable; so, rather than commit himself to his logic of the aesthetic sign as a designation of a value which cannot be located and which thus cannot be an interest-value, he offers us the ordinary procedure of positivism; that is to say, he shows us how we may reduce the aesthetic sign to a *denotatum* after all.

Since a statement must say something about something, it must involve signs for locating what is referred to, and such signs are ultimately indexical signs [i.e., "pointing" signs]. An iconic sign in isolation cannot then be a statement, and a work of art, conceived as an iconic sign, cannot be true in the semantical sense of the term. Nevertheless, the statement that a work of art is "true" might under analysis turn out to be an elliptical form of syntactical, semantical, or pragmatical statements. Thus semantically it might be intended to affirm that the work in question actually is iconic of the value structure of a certain object or situation. . . .

The work of art is elliptical and iconic; that is, it is an image from which the semantical dimension is omitted, or in which it remains vague. By translating the icon, by expanding it and filling it in with a *denotatum,* we construct a situation external to the work of art: a situation which replaces it. In the usual terms of literary criticism, this situation is the "subject" which exists outside the language of the poem. For the language is merely "iconic of" this ordinary prose subject.

So a neo-classical theory of poetic language not only gave the case for poetry away to the scientist; it has become the foundation of the scientists' theory of poetry. When Mr. Richards remarked, in *Science and Poetry,* that we were now getting on a large scale "genuine knowledge" which would soon reduce poetry to the level of the "pseudo-statement," we could not see how right he was.

Right—from the point of view of neo-classical theory. So long as the scientific procedure was observation, description, and classification, it was not very different from the procedure of common sense and its feeling for the reality of ordinary experience. As late as the first edition (1892) of *The Grammar of Science,* Karl Pearson said: "The aesthetic judgment pronounces for or against the interpretation of the creative imagination according as that interpretation embodies or contradicts the phenomena of life, which we ourselves have observed." But from the point of view of Unified Science, this principle of common-sense observation will no longer serve; it does not go far enough. And so we have a dilemma. Since the language of poetry can be shown to be not strictly relevant to objects and situations as these are presented by the positivist techniques, poetry becomes either nonsense or hortatory rhetoric.

The semiotic approach to aesthetics "has the merit of concreteness"; yet we have seen that Mr. Morris never quite gets around to a definite work of art. In *Science, Art, and Technology,* he distinguishes three primary forms of discourse and relates them to the three dimensions of semiosis:

1. Scientific discourse: semantical dimension.
2. Aesthetic discourse: syntactical dimension.
3. Technological discourse: pragmatical dimension.

We have seen that the iconic sign is semantically weak; so the aesthetic sign, a variety of iconic sign, must function

primarily at the syntactical level; that is, if we look at it
"indexically" it "points" first of all to itself. Looking at
the aesthetic sign from this point of view, we are forced
to see that it wholly lacks cognitive content, and it is subject to the operation of "transformation rules." Does the
"concreteness" of the semiotic approach to art consist in
this? Again, is the syntactical dimension that in which
direct apprehension of the aesthetic sign is possible? Once
more it must be said that this direct apprehension seems
impossible unless there is an agency of apprehension—a
knowing mind; without this we get only an "interpretant,"
which is conceivable only at the pragmatic level; and if
the interpretant is intelligible, it is so in terms of semantical relevance, or of the scientific form of discourse. For
Mr. Morris himself confesses: ". . . in so far as the knowledge of value which art gives is the more than the having
of value [i.e., is the *knowing* of value] there is no reason
to suppose that this knowledge is *other than scientific in
character.*"

It is significant here that Mr. Morris conceives the character of poetry in the relation of pragmatics and semantics.
What is our response to poetry and how do we behave
when we read it: what, in a word, does it lead to? There
is a certain uneasy piety in the extravagant claim that
poetry is the realm of values; and there is no way, I think,
to get around the conclusion that, since the values are not
attached to reality, they are irresponsible feelings. They
are, in fact, rhetoric. And it is also significant that for Mr.
Morris the study of rhetoric is a branch of pragmatics; it

is even a kind of technological instrument. For, in the essay, "Science, Art, and Technology," poetry seems to acquire its main reponsibility in the technological function of telling us what we *ought* to want and do. Here again neo-classical didacticism appears in terms of a rigorous instrumentalism.

Does the language of poetry mean what it says, or does it mean the "situation" that we get from it in a process of reduction? Although we have seen Mr. Morris's bias, we have also seen that he has not made up his mind: he would like to have it both ways. The origin of this dilemma is remote. But there is always "the sad ghost of Coleridge beckoning from the shades."

IV

The famous Chapter XIV of *Biographia Literaria* has been the background of the criticism of poetry for more than a hundred years. Its direct influence has been very great; its indirect influence, through Poe upon Baudelaire, and through the French symbolists down to contemporary English and American poets, has perhaps been even greater. This chapter is the most influential statement on poetry ever formulated by an English critic: its insights, when we have them, are ours, and ours too its contradictions. Yet the remarkable "definition" of poetry, which I shall now quote, is not, as we shall presently see, the chief source of the aesthetic dilemma that we inherit today. (That source is another passage.) Here is the definition:

A poem is that species of composition, which is opposed to works of science, by proposing for its *immediate* object pleasure, not truth; and from all other species—(having this object in common with it)—it is distinguished by proposing to itself such delight from the *whole,* as is compatible with a distinct gratification from each component *part.*

Much of the annoyance and misunderstanding caused by this passage has not been Coleridge's fault; but is rather due to the failure of literary men to observe the accurate use of *species.* For Coleridge is giving us a strict Aristotelian definition of a *species* within a given *genus.* It is not a qualitative statement, and it does not answer the question: *What* is poetry? The *whatness* of poetry does not come within the definition; and I believe that nowhere else does Coleridge offer us an explicit qualitative distinction between poetry and other "species of composition" which may be "opposed" to it.

For what is Coleridge saying? (I have never seen a literal reading of the passage by any critic.) There is the generic division: composition. A poem is a species within the genus; but so is a work of science. How are the two species distinguished? By their immediate objects. It is curious that Coleridge phrases the passage as if a poem were a person "proposing" to himself a certain end, pleasure; so for *object* we have got to read *effect.* A poem, then, differs from a work of science in its immediate effect upon us; and that immediate effect is pleasure. But other species of composition may aim at the effect of pleasure. A poem differs from these in the relation of part to whole: the parts must give us a distinct pleasure, moment by moment, and they are not to be conceived as subordinate to the whole; they make up the whole.

If there is an objective relation of part to whole, Coleridge does not say what it is; nor does he distinguish that relation in terms of any specific poetic work. It is strictly a quantitative analogy taken, perhaps, from geometry. And the only purpose it serves is this: in the paragraph following the "definition" he goes on to say that "the philosophic critics of all ages coincide" in asserting that beautiful, isolated lines or distichs are not a poem, and that neither is "an unsustained composition" of uninteresting parts a *"legitimate* poem." What we have here, then, is a sound but ordinary critical insight; but because it is merely an extension of the pleasure principle implicit in the "definition," we are not prepared by it to distinguish objectively a poem from any other form of expression. The distinction lies in the effect, and it is a psychological effect. In investigating the differentia of poetry—as Mr. Morris would put it—we are eventually led away from the poem into what has been known since Coleridge's time as the psychology of poetry.

The difficulties of this theory Coleridge seems not to have been aware of; yet he illustrates them perfectly. In the second paragraph after the famous definition he writes this remarkable passage:

The first chapter of Isaiah—(indeed a very large portion of the whole book)—is poetry in the most emphatic sense; yet it would be no less irrational than strange to assert, that pleasure, not truth, was the immediate object of the prophet. In short, whatever specific import we attach to the word, Poetry, there will be found involved in it, as a necessary consequence, that a poem of any length neither can be, nor ought to be, all poetry. Yet if an harmonious whole is to be produced, the remaining parts must be preserved in keeping with the poetry; and this can no otherwise be effected than by such a studied selection and artificial arrangement, as will partake of one, though not a peculiar property of poetry. And this again can be no other than the property of exciting a more continuous and equal attention than the language of prose aims at, whether colloquial or written.

This is probably the most confused statement ever uttered by a great critic, and it has probably done more damage to critical thought than anything else said by any critic. Isaiah is poetry in "the most emphatic sense," although his immediate object (effect) is truth. It will be observed that, whereas in the definition our attention is drawn to a species of composition, a poem, we are here confronted with the personage, Isaiah, who does have the power of proposing an object; and Isaiah's immediate object is truth. But are we to suppose that the effect of the poem and the object of the prophet are to be apprehended in the same way? Is our experience of truth the same as our experience of pleasure? If there is a difference between truth and pleasure, and if an immediate effect of pleasure is the specific "property" of poetry (how a property can be an effect it is difficult to see), how can the first chapter of Isaiah be poetry at all? It cannot be, looked at in these terms; and as a matter of fact Coleridge rather slyly withdraws his compliment to Isaiah when he goes on to say that a "poem of any length neither can be, nor ought to be, all poetry." Isaiah is not all poetry; he is partly truth, or even mostly truth. And the element of truth, while it is strictly speaking insubordinate and unassimilable, can be used by means of an artificial arrangement—meter. There is no doubt that meter does on the whole what Coleridge attributes to it: it demands a "continuous and equal attention." Does he mean to say that the insubordinate element of truth—insubordinate to the immediate effect of pleasure—should be given such conspicuous emphasis? Or does he perhaps mean that the attention will be fixed upon the metrical pattern, so that the nonpoetic element will be less conspicuous?

Coleridge's theory of meter is not quite pertinent here: in the later and more elaborate discussion of meter in *Biographia Literaria* there is the general conclusion that meter is indispensable to poetry. In Chapter XIV, now being examined, he speaks of meter as "an artificial arrangement ... not a peculiar property of poetry."

There is, then, in Coleridge's poetic theory a persistent dilemma. *He cannot make up his mind whether the specifically poetic element is an objective feature of the poem, or is distinguishable only as a subjective effect.* He cannot, in short, choose between metaphysics and psychology. His general emphasis is psychological, with metaphysical ambiguities.

The distinction between Fancy and Imagination is ultimately a psychological one: he discusses the problem in terms of separate faculties, and the objective poetical properties, presumably resulting from the use of these faculties, are never defined, but are given only occasional illustration. (I have in mind his magnificent analysis of "Venus and Adonis," the value of which lies less perhaps in the critical principles he supposes he is illustrating, than in the perfect taste with which he selects the good passages for admiration.) When Coleridge speaks of the "esemplastic power" of the Imagination, it is always a "faculty" of the mind, not an objective poetic order. When he says that a poem gives us "a more than usual state of emotion with more than usual order," we acknowledge the fact, without being able to discern in the merely comparative degree of the adjective the fundamental difference between the poetic and the philosophic powers which Coleridge frequently asserts, but which he nowhere objectively establishes. The psychological bias of his "system" is perfectly revealed in this summary passage of Chapter XIV:

My own conclusions on the nature of poetry, in the strictest use of the word, have been in part anticipated in some of the remarks on the Fancy and Imagination in the early part of this work. What is poetry?—is so nearly the same question with, what is a poet?—that the answer to the one is involved in the solution to the other. For it is a distinction resulting from the poetic genius itself, which sustains and modifies the images, thoughts, and emotions of the poet's own mind.

There can be little doubt that Coleridge's failure to get out of the dilemma of Intellect-or-Feeling has been passed on to us as a fatal legacy. If the first object of poetry is an effect, and if that effect is pleasure, does it not necessarily follow that truth and knowledge may be better set forth in some other order altogether? It is true that Coleridge made extravagant claims for a poetic order of truth, and it is upon these claims that Mr. I. A. Richards has based his fine book, *Coleridge on the Imagination*: Mr. Richards's own testimony is that the claims were not coherent. The coherent part of Coleridge's theory is the fatal dilemma that I have described. Truth is only the secondary consideration of the poet, and from the point of view of positivism the knowledge, or truth, that poetry gives us is immature and inadequate. What of the primary consideration of the poet—pleasure?

Pleasure is the single qualitative feature of Coleridge's famous definition; but it is not *in* the definition objectively. And with the development of modern psychology it has ceased to be qualitative, even subjectively. It is a *response*. The fate of Coleridge's system, then, has been its gradual extinction in the terminology of experimental psychology. The poetry has been extinguished in the poet. The poetic "effect" is a "response" to a "stimulus"; and in the early works of Mr. Richards we get for the first time the questions, rigorously applied: Is the poetic response relevant to the real world? Is it relevant to action? Poetry has come under the general idea of "operational validity." So we must turn briefly to Mr. Richards.

V

In *Science and Poetry* (1926) Mr. Richards condensed in untechnical language the position that he had set forth in detail earlier, in *The Principles of Literary Criticism*. The positivist side of Mr. Richards's thought at that time is plainly revealed in a passage like this:

You contrive not to laugh [in church]; but there is no doubt about the activity of the impulses in their restricted form. The much more subtle and elaborate impulses which a poem excites are not different in principle. *They do not show themselves as a rule, they do not come out into the open, largely because they are so complex.* [Italics mine.] When they have adjusted themselves to one another and become organized into a coherent whole, the needs concerned may be satisfied. *In a fully developed man a state of readiness for action will take the place of action when the full appropriate situation for action is not present.*[6] [Mr. Richards's italics.]

The mere state of readiness for action is the poetic experience in terms of value and relevance. The readiness points to the "direct apprehension" of an interest-value in Mr. Morris's sense; but the failure of the action to come off, the lack of the "full appropriate situation for action," indicates the absence of a *denotatum*. We receive the designation of a value without being provided with a situation in which we can act upon it. The remarkable parallel between Mr. Richards's early theories of poetry and the re-

[6] *Science and Poetry*, pp. 28-29.

cent theories of Mr. Morris need not detain us. It is enough to point out that Mr. Richards anticipated fifteen years ago everything that Mr. Morris's science of semiotic has to say about the language of poetry.

I have italicized a sentence, in the quotation from Mr. Richards, for two reasons: first, the vagueness óf the language is significant; secondly, the idea of the coherent whole into which the "impulses" are organized has no experimental basis in terms of impulses. Mr. John Crowe Ransom remarks that Mr. Richards never shows us *how* this ordering act of poetry upon our minds takes place, and then proceeds to discern the reason for Mr. Richards's vague statements about the conduct of poetic stimulation and response:

Most readers will retort, of course, that in the very large majority of cases the spiritual happenings are the only happenings we have observed, and *the neural happenings are simply what the behaviorists would like to observe.* [Italics mine.] At present the mental datum is the fact and the neural datum is the inference.[7]

In throwing out the mental fact Mr. Richards in his early writings preceded Mr. Morris in his rejection of the cognitive powers of the mind. I do not suggest any direct influence from Mr. Richards upon Mr. Morris, although Mr. Morris has acknowledged the work of his predecessor: it is easier to relate these men to a much wider movement.

[7] "A Psychologist Looks at Poetry," *The World's Body*, p. 147. This essay is the most searching examination of Mr. Richards's position—or positions—that I have seen.

That movement is positivism, and it is more than a strict scientific method.

It is a general attitude towards experience. If it is not, why should Mr. Richards have attempted in his early criticism to represent the total poetic experience and even the structure of poetry in one of the positivist languages— experimental psychology? It was representation by analogy. The experimental basis for such a representation was wholly lacking. Mr. Richards, had we listened hard enough, was saying in *The Principles of Literary Criticism* and *Science and Poetry* that here at last is what poetry would be if we could only reduce it to the same laboratory technique that we use in psychology; and without warning to the unwary reader, whose credulity was already prepared by his own positivist *zeitgeist,* Mr. Richards went on to state "results" that looked like the result of an experiment; but the experiment had never been made. It had been inferred. The "impulses" that we feel in response to a poem, says Mr. Richards, "do not show themselves as a rule." There is no scientific evidence that they have ever shown themselves to Mr. Richards or to anybody else. Mr. Richards like a good positivist was the victim of a deep-seated compulsive analogy, an elusive but all-engrossing assumption that all experience can be reduced to what is actually the very limited frame of reference supplied by a doctrine of correlation, or of the relevance of stimulus to response. This early procedure of Mr. Richards's was not even empiricism, for in empiricism the cognitive intelligence is not eliminated in the pursuit of verifiable facts.

Mr. Richards, like Mr. Morris after him, eliminated cognition without demonstrating experimentally the *data* of his behavioristic poetics. So this doctrine was not empiricism: it came out of the demi-religion of positivism. The poetry had been absorbed into a pseudo-scientific jargon, no more "relevant" to poetry than the poetic pseudo-statement was relevant to the world: the net result was zero from both points of view.

I have put this brief commentary on Mr. Richards's early poetics in the past tense because it is no longer his poetics. From 1926, the year of *Science and Poetry,* he has come a long way. It is perhaps not an extravagant claim to make for Mr. Richards's intellectual history, that it will probably turn out to be the most instructive, among critics, of our age. His great intellectual powers, his learning, his devotion to poetry—a devotion somewhat frustrated but as marked fifteen years ago as now—are qualities of an intellectual honesty rare in any age. In exactly ten years, from 1926, he arrived, in *The Philosophy of Rhetoric* (1936), at such a statement as this:

So far from verbal language being a "compromise for a language of intuition"—a thin, but better-than-nothing, substitute for real experience—language, well used, is a *completion* and does what the intuitions of sensation by themselves cannot do. Words are the meeting points at which regions of experience which can never combine in sensation or intuition, come together. They are the occasion and means of that growth which is the mind's endless endeavor to order itself. That is why we have language. *It is no mere signalling system* [Italics mine]. It is the instrument of all our distinctively human development, of everything in which we go beyond the animals. [Pp. 130-131.]

These words should be read and re-read with the greatest care by critics who still cite the early Richards as the continuing head of a positivist tradition in criticism. There is, in this passage, first of all, an implicit repudiation of the leading doctrine of *The Principles of Literary Criticism*. The early doctrine did look upon poetic language as a "substitute for real experience," if by experience is meant responses relevant to scientifically ascertained facts and situations: this early doctrine, as I have indicated, anticipated in psychological terms Mr. Morris's poetic doctrine of designation without *denotatum*, of value without consummation of value, of interpretant without an interpreter. Mr. Richards's more familiar equivalents of the semiotic terms were: pseudo-statement without referents; poetry as the orderer of our minds, as the valuer, although the ordering mysteriously operated in fictions irrelevant to the real world; a response, a behavioristic "readiness for action," without a knowing mind.

Language, says Mr. Richards, "is no mere signalling system." With that sentence the early psychological doctrine is discreetly put away. Is it too much to assume that the adjective "signalling" may indicate the relation of Mr. Richards's present views to the pragmatic bias of Mr. Morris's aesthetics? He speaks of the inadequacy of "sensation" and "intuition," and of the equal inadequacy of "intuitions of sensation." Is not the mere sensation Mr. Morris's interpretant, the intuition of sensation his iconic sign? What is the "completion" which language "well used" can achieve beyond sensation and intuition?

It is doubtless knowledge of a kind that we can discuss only if we assume the action of a knowing mind. Of what is it the completion? In the paragraph following the passage that I have just quoted, Mr. Richards cites Coleridge:

Are not words parts and germinations of the plant? And what is the law of their growth? In something of this sort I would destroy the old antithesis of Words and Things: elevating, as it were, Words into Things and living things too.

This attribution to the language of poetry of a special kind of "life" goes back to Mr. Richards's *Coleridge on the Imagination* (1935), the most ambitious attempt of a modern critic to force into unity the antithesis of language and subject, of pleasure and truth. It is an antithesis which, as we have seen, has harassed critical theory since the time of Coleridge. Mr. Richards's book may be looked upon as an effort to finish Coleridge's own uncompleted struggle with this neo-classical dilemma. This is not the place to describe the entire nature and scope of his effort, or to estimate it. A single chapter of the book, "The Wind Harp," contains the clearest presentation of the antithesis that I have seen by a modern critic.

There are "two doctrines," he says, which have tended to flourish independently—"And yet, neither is intelligible, apart from Imagination." He continues:

The two doctrines can be stated as follows:

1. The mind of the poet at moments ... gains an insight into reality, reads Nature as a symbol of something behind or within Nature not ordinarily perceived.

2. The mind of the poet creates a Nature into which his own feelings, his aspirations and apprehensions, are projected.

Now the positivist sciences have denied all validity to the first doctrine: as a proposition, in the many forms in which it may be stated, it is strictly meaningless. For the sole effective procedure towards nature is the positivist. The second doctrine is the standard poetics of our time: projection of feeling. The confusion and contradiction that we saw in Mr. Morris and in the early Richards came of trying to square a theory of interest-value with a theory of emotional projection which was not firmly based upon positivist knowledge. That contradiction is the clue to the "unintelligibility" of the doctrines if held separately. If you take the first alone, eliminating the second, you eliminate the "mind," and you get pure positivism: in thus eliminating cognition you lose "everything in which we go beyond the animals." If you take the second alone, and eliminate the external world in any of the four meanings [8] that Mr. Richards gives to the phrase, you have a knowing mind without anything that it can know.

Before the development of the positivist procedures towards nature, the pressure of this dilemma was not seriously felt. We have seen in Matthew Arnold (the determined anti-dialectician) the belief that the subject is

[8] *Coleridge on the Imagination,* pp. 157-8.

external to the language—a merely common-sense view inherited from neo-classical theory. The poetic subject was
the world of ordinary experience; but as soon as the subject—Nature—became the field of positivism, the language
of poetry ceased to represent it; ceased, in fact, to have
any validity, or to set forth anything real. (The world of
positivism is a world without minds to know the world;
and yet Mr. Morris does not hesitate to assert that his
Unified Science will save the world. For whom will it be
saved?)

What is this Imagination which Mr. Richards says will
make the two doctrines intelligible? No doubt it becomes
in his hands something different from Coleridge's conception of it: it closely resembles an Hegelian synthesis,
which joins the opposites in a new proposition in which
their truths, no longer contradictory, are preserved.

They are [says Mr. Richards of the two doctrines] neither
consequences of *a priori* decisions, nor verifiable as the empirical statements of science are verifiable; and all verifiable
statements are independent of them. But this does not dimin-
ish in the least their interest, or that of the other senses in
which they may be true.

With that we are almost ready to leave Mr. Richards,
who offers no final solution of the problem of the unified
imagination. "It is the privilege of poetry," he says finely,
"to preserve us from mistaking our notions either for
things or for ourselves. *Poetry is the completest mode of
utterance.*" [9] It is neither the world of verifiable science

9 *Ibid.,* p. 163.

nor a projection of ourselves; yet it is *complete*. And because it is complete knowledge we may, I think, claim
for it a unique kind of responsibility, and see in it at
times an irresponsibility equally distinct. The order of
completeness that it achieves in the great works of the
imagination is not the order of experimental completeness
aimed at by the positivist sciences, whose responsibility is
directed towards the verification of limited techniques.
The completeness of science is an abstraction covering an
ideal of co-operation among specialized methods. No one
can have an experience of science, or of a single science.
For the completeness of *Hamlet* is not of the experimental
order, but of the experienced order: it is, in short, of the
mythical order. And here Mr. Richards can give us a final
insight. Myths, he says,

...are no amusement or diversion to be sought as a relaxa-
tion and an escape from the hard realities of life. They are
these hard realities in projection, their symbolic recognition,
co-ordination and acceptance.... The opposite and discordant
qualities in things in them acquire a form.... Without his
mythologies man is only a cruel animal without a soul...a
congeries of possibilities without order and aim.[10]

Man, without his mythologies, is an interpretant. Mr.
Richards's books may be seen together as a parable, as a
mythical and dramatic projection, of the failure of the
modern mind to understand poetry on the assumptions
underlying the demi-religion of positivism. We do not

[10] *Ibid.*, pp. 171-172.

need to reject the positive and rational mode of inquiry into poetry; yet even from Mr. Morris we get the warning lest we substitute the criticism for the poem, and thus commit ourselves to a "learned ignorance." We must return to, we must never leave, the poem itself. Its "interest" value is a cognitive one; it is sufficient that here, in the poem, we get knowledge of a whole object. If rational inquiry is the only mode of criticism, we must yet remember that the way we employ that mode must always powerfully affect our experience of the poem. I have been concerned in this commentary with the compulsive, almost obsessed, application of an all-engrossing principle of pragmatic reduction to a formed realm of our experience, the distinction of which is its complete knowledge, the full body of the experience that it offers us. However we may see the completeness of poetry, it is a problem less to be solved than, in its full import, to be preserved.

TENSION IN POETRY

I

MANY POEMS that we ordinarily think of as good poetry—and some, besides, that we neglect—have certain common features that will allow us to invent, for their sharper apprehension, the name of a single quality. I shall call that quality tension. In abstract language, a poetic work has distinct quality as the ultimate effect of the whole, and that whole is the "result" of a configuration of meaning which it is the duty of the critic to examine and evaluate. In setting forth this duty as my present procedure I am trying to amplify a critical approach that I have used on other occasions, without wholly giving up the earlier method, which I should describe as the analysis of the general ideas implicit in the poetic work.

Towards the end of this essay I shall cite examples of "tension," but I shall not say that they exemplify tension only, or that other qualities must be ignored. There are all kinds of poetry, as many as there are good poets, as many even as there are good poems, for poets may be expected to write more than one kind of poetry; and no single critical insight may impute an exclusive validity to any one kind. In all ages there are schools demanding that one sort only be written—their sort: political poetry for the sake of the cause; picturesque poetry for the sake of the home town; didactic poetry for the sake of the parish; even a generalized personal poetry for the sake of the reassurance and safety of numbers. This last I suppose is the most common variety, the anonymous lyricism in which the common personality exhibits its commonness, its obscure and standard eccentricity, in a language that seems always to be deteriorating; so that today many poets are driven to inventing private languages, or very narrow ones, because public speech has become heavily tainted with mass feeling.

Mass language is the medium of "communication," and its users are less interested in bringing to formal order what is today called the "affective state" than in arousing that state.

Once you have said that everything is One it is obvious that literature is the same as propaganda; once you have said that no truth can be known apart from the immediate dialectical process of history it is obvious that all contemporary artists must prepare the same fashionplate. It is clear too that the One is limited in space as well as time, and the no less Hegelian Fascists are right in saying that all art is patriotic.

What Mr. William Empson calls patriotic poetry sings not merely in behalf of the State; you will find it equally in a lady-like lyric and in much of the political poetry of our time. It is the poetry of the mass language, very different from the "language of the people" which interested the late W. B. Yeats. For example:

What from the splendid dead
We have inherited—
Furrows sweet to the grain, and the weed subdued—
See now the slug and the mildew plunder.
Evil does overwhelm
The larkspur and the corn;
We have seen them go under.

From this stanza by Miss Millay we infer that her splendid ancestors made the earth a good place that has somehow gone bad—and you get the reason from the title: "Justice Denied in Massachusetts." How Massachusetts could cause a general dessication, why (as we are told in a footnote to the poem) the execution of Sacco and Vanzetti should have anything to do with the rotting of the crops, it is never made clear. These lines are mass language: they arouse an affective state in one set of terms, and suddenly an object quite unrelated to those terms gets the benefit of it; and this effect, which is usually achieved, as I think it is here, without conscious effort, is sentimentality. Miss Millay's poem was admired when it first appeared about ten years ago, and is no doubt still admired, by persons to whom it communicates certain feelings about social justice, by persons for whom the lines are the occasion of feelings shared by them and the poet. But if you do not share those feelings, as I happen not to share them in the images of dessicated nature, the lines and even the entire poem are impenetrably obscure.

I am attacking here the fallacy of communication in

poetry. (I am not attacking social justice.) It is no less a fallacy in the writing of poetry than of critical theory. The critical doctrine fares ill the further back you apply it; I suppose one may say—if one wants a landmark—that it began to prosper after 1798; for on the whole nineteenth-century English verse is a poetry of communication. The poets were trying to use verse to convey ideas and feelings that they secretly thought could be better conveyed by science (consult Shelley's *Defense*), or by what today we call, in a significantly bad poetic phrase, the Social Sciences. Yet possibly because the poets believed the scientists to be tough, and the poets joined the scientists in thinking the poets tender, the poets stuck to verse. It may hardly be said that we change this tradition of poetic futility by giving it a new name, Social Poetry. May a poet hope to deal more adequately with sociology than with physics? If he seizes upon either at the level of scientific procedure, has he not abdicated his position as poet?

At a level of lower historical awareness than that exhibited by Mr. Edmund Wilson's later heroes of the Symbolist school, we find the kind of verse that I have been quoting, verse long ago intimidated by the pseudo-rationalism of the Social Sciences. This sentimental intimidation has been so complete that, however easy the verse looked on the page, it gave up all claim to sense. (I assume here what I cannot now demonstrate, that Miss Millay's poem is obscure but that Donne's "Second Anniversarie" is not.) As another example of this brand of obscurity I have selected at random a nineteenth-century lyric, "The Vine," by James Thomson:

> *The wine of love is music,*
>   *And the feast of love is song:*
> *When love sits down to banquet,*
>   *Love sits long:*
>
> *Sits long and rises drunken,*
>   *But not with the feast and the wine;*
> *He reeleth with his own heart,*
>   *That great rich Vine.*

The language here appeals to an existing affective state; it has no coherent meaning either literally or in terms of ambiguity or implication; it may be wholly replaced by any of its several paraphrases, which are already latent in our minds. One of these is the confused image of a self-intoxicating man-about-town. Now good poetry can bear the closest literal examination of every phrase, and is its own safeguard against our irony. But the more closely we examine this lyric, the more obscure it becomes; the more we trace the implications of the imagery, the denser the confusion. The imagery adds nothing to the general idea that it tries to sustain; it even deprives that idea of the dignity it has won at the hands of a long succession of better poets going back, I suppose, to Guinizelli:

> *Al cor gentil ripara sempre Amore*
> *Come alla selva augello in la verdura . . .*

What I want to make clear is the particular kind of failure, not the degree, in a certain kind of poetry. Were we interested in degrees we might give comfort to the nineteenth century by citing lines from John Cleveland or Abraham Cowley, bad lyric verse no better than "The Vine," written in an age that produced some of the greatest English poetry. Here are some lines from Cowley's "Hymn: to light," a hundred-line inventory of some of the offices performed by the subject in a universe that still seems to be on the whole Ptolemaic; I should not care to guess the length the poem might have reached under the Copernican system. Here is one of the interesting duties of light:

> *Nor amidst all these Triumphs does thou scorn*
> *The humble glow-worm to adorn,*
> *And with those living spangles gild,*
> *(O Greatness without Pride!) the Bushes of the Field.*

Again:

> *The Violet, springs little Infant, stands,*
> *Girt in thy purple Swadling-bands:*
> *On the fair Tulip thou dost dote;*
> *Thou cloath'st it in a gay and party-colour'd Coat.*

This, doubtless, is metaphysical poetry; however bad the lines may be—they are pretty bad—they have no qualities, bad or good, in common with "The Vine." Mr. Ransom has given us, in a remarkable essay, "Shakespeare at Sonnets" (*The World's Body*, 1938), an excellent description of this kind of poetry: "The impulse to metaphysical poetry . . . consists in committing the feelings in the case . . . to their determination within the elected figure." That is to say, in metaphysical poetry the logical order is explicit; it must be coherent; the imagery by which it is sensuously embodied must have at least the appearance of logical determinism: perhaps the appearance only, because the varieties of ambiguity and contradiction possible beneath the logical surface are endless, as Mr. Empson has demonstrated in his elucidation of Marvel's "The Garden." Here it is enough to say that the development of imagery by extension, its logical determinants being an Ariadne's thread that the poet will not permit us to lose, is the leading feature of the poetry called metaphysical.

But to recognize it is not to evaluate it; and I take it that Mr. Ransom was giving us a true Aristotelian definition of a genus, in which the identification of a type does not compel us to discern the implied values. Logical extension of imagery is no doubt the key to the meaning of Donne's "Valediction: forbidding mourning"; it may equally initiate inquiry into the ludicrous failure of "Hymn: to light," to which I will now return.

While "The Vine" and "Hymn: to light" seem to me equally bad poetry, Cowley's failure is somewhat to be preferred; its negative superiority lies in a firmer use of the language. There is no appeal to an affective state; the leading statement can be made perfectly explicit: God is light, and light is life. The poem is an analytical proposition exhibiting the properties inherent in the major term; that is, exhibiting as much of the universe as Cowley could get around to before he wearied of logical extension. But I think it is possible to infer that good poetry could have been written in Cowley's language; and we know that it was. Every term, even the verbs converted into nouns, denotes an object, and in the hands of a good poet would be amenable to controlled distortions of literal representation. But here the distortions are uncontrolled. Everything is in this language that a poet needs except the poetry, or the imagination, or what I shall presently illustrate under the idea of tension.

I have called "Hymn: to light" an analytical proposition. That is the form in which the theme must have appeared to Cowley's mind; that is to say, simple analysis of the term, *God,* gave him, as it gave everybody else in Christendom, the proposition: God is light. (Perhaps, under neo-Platonic influence, the prime Christian symbol, as Professor Fletcher and others have shown in reducing to their sources the powers of the Three Blessed Ladies of *The Divine Comedy.*) But in order to write his poem Cowley had to develop the symbol by synthetic accretion, by adding to light properties not inherent in its simple analysis:

> *The Violet, springs little Infant, stands,*
> *Girt in thy purple Swadling-bands . . .*

The image, such as it is, is an addition to the central figure of light, an assertion of a hitherto undetected relation among the objects, light, diapers, and violets—a miscellany that I recommend to the consideration of Mr. E. E. Cummings, who could get something out of it that Cowley did not intend us to get. If you will think again of "The Vine," you will observe that Thomson permits, in the opposite direction, an equal license with the objects *de*noted by his imagery, with the unhappy results that we have already seen.

"The Vine" is a failure in denotation. "Hymn: to light" is a failure in connotation. The language of "The Vine" lacks objective content. Take "music" and "song" in the first two lines; the context does not allow us to apprehend the terms in extension; that is, there is no reference to objects that we may distinguish as "music" and "song"; the wine of love could have as well been song, its feast music. In "Hymn: to light," a reduction to their connotations of the terms *violet, swadling-bands,* and *light* (the last being represented by the pronoun *thou*) yields a clutter of images that may be unified only if we forget the firm denotations of the terms. If we are going to receive as valid the infancy of the violet, we have to ignore the metaphor that conveys it, for the metaphor renders the violet absurd; by ignoring the diaper, and the two terms associated with it, we cease to read the passage, and begin for ourselves the building up of acceptable denotations for the terms of the metaphor.

Absurd: but on what final ground I call these poems absurd I cannot state as a principle. I appeal to the reader's experience, and invite him to form a judgment of my own. It is easy enough to say, as I shall say in detail in a moment, that good poetry is a unity of all the meanings from the furthest extremes of intension and extension. Yet our recognition of the action of this unified meaning is the gift of experience, of culture, of, if you will, our humanism. Our powers of discrimination are not deductive powers, though they may be aided by them; they wait rather upon the cultivation of our total human powers, and they represent a special application of those powers to a single medium of experience—poetry.

I have referred to a certain kind of poetry as the embodiment of the fallacy of communication: it is a poetry that communicates the affective state, which (in terms of language) results from the irresponsible denotations of words. There is a vague grasp of the "real" world. The history of this fallacy, which is as old as poetry but which towards the end of the eighteenth century began to dominate not only poetry, but other arts as well—its history would probably show that the poets gave up the language of denotation to the scientists, and kept for themselves a continually thinning flux of peripheral connotations. The companion fallacy, to which I can give only the literal name, the fallacy of mere denotation, I have also illustrated from Cowley: this is the poetry which contradicts our most developed human insights in so far as it fails to use and direct the rich connotation with which language has been informed by experience.

II

We return to the inquiry set for this discussion: to find out whether there is not a more central achievement in poetry than that represented by either of the extreme examples that we have been considering. I proposed as descriptive of that achievement, the term *tension*. I am using the term not as a general metaphor, but as a special one, derived from lopping the prefixes off the logical terms *ex*tension and *in*tension. What I am saying, of course, is that the meaning of poetry is its "tension," the full organized body of all the extension and intension that we can find in it. The remotest figurative significance that we can derive does not invalidate the extensions of the literal statement. Or we may begin with the literal statement and by stages develop the complications of metaphor: at every stage we may pause to state the meaning so far apprehended, and at every stage the meaning will be coherent.

The meanings that we select at different points along the infinite line between extreme intension and extreme extension will vary with our personal "drive," or "interest," or "approach": the Platonist will tend to stay pretty close to the end of the line where extension, and simple abstraction of the object into a universal, is easiest, for he will be a fanatic in morals or some kind of works, and will insist upon the shortest way with what will ever appear to him the dissenting ambiguities at the intensive end of the scale. The Platonist (I do not say that his opponent is the Aristotelian) might decide that Marvel's "To His Coy Mistress" recommends immoral behavior to the young men, in whose behalf he would try to suppress the poem. That, of course, would be one "true" meaning of "To His Coy Mistress," but it is a meaning that the full tension of the poem will not allow us to entertain exclusively. For we are compelled, since it is there, to give equal weight to an intensive meaning so rich that, without contradicting the literal statement of the lover-mistress convention, it lifts that convention into an insight into one phase of the human predicament—the conflict of sensuality and asceticism.

I should like to quote now, not from Marvel, but a stanza from Donne that I hope will reinforce a little what I have just said and connect it with some earlier remarks.

> *Our two soules therefore, which are one,*
> *Though I must goe, endure not yet*
> *A breach, but an expansion,*
> *Like gold to aiery thinnesse beate.*

Here Donne brings together the developing imagery of twenty lines under the implicit proposition: the unity of two lovers' souls is a nonspatial entity, and is therefore indivisible. That, I believe, is what Mr. John Crowe Ransom would call the logic of the passage; it is the abstract form of its extensive meaning. Now the interesting feature here is the logical contradiction of embodying the unitary, nonspatial soul in a spatial image: the malleable gold is a plane whose surface can always be extended mathematically by one-half, towards infinity; the souls are this infinity. The finite image of the gold, in extension, logically contradicts the intensive meaning (infinity) which it conveys; but it does not invalidate that meaning. We have seen that Cowley compelled us to ignore the denoted diaper in order that we might take seriously the violet which it pretended to swathe. But in Donne's "Valediction: forbidding mourning" the clear denotation of the gold contains, by intension, the full meaning of the passage. If we reject the gold, we reject the meaning, for the meaning is wholly absorbed into the image of the gold. Intension and extension are here one, and they enrich each other.

Before I leave this beautiful object, I should like to notice two incidental features in further proof of Donne's mastery. "Expansion"—a term denoting an abstract property common to many objects, perhaps here one property of a gas: it expands visibly the quality of the beaten gold.

> ... *endure not yet*
> *a breach* ...

But if the lovers' souls are the formidable, inhuman entity that we have seen, are they not superior to the contingency of a breach? Yes and no: both answers are true answers; for by means of the sly "yet" Donne subtly guards himself against our irony, which would otherwise be quick to scrutinize the extreme metaphor. The lovers have not en-

dured a breach, but they are simple, miserable human beings, and they may quarrel tomorrow.[1]

Now all this meaning and more, and it is all one meaning, is embedded in that stanza: I say more because I have
not exhausted the small fraction of significance that my
limited powers have permitted me to see. For example, I
have not discussed the rhythm, which is of the essential
meaning; I have violently isolated four lines from the
meaning of the whole poem. Yet, fine as it is, I do not
think the poem the greatest poetry; perhaps only very
little of Donne makes that grade, or of anybody else.
Donne offers many examples of tension in imagery, easier
for the expositor than greater passages in Shakespeare.

But convenience of elucidation is not a canon of criticism. I wish now to introduce other kinds of instance, and
to let them stand for us as a sort of Arnoldish touchstones
to the perfection that poetic statement has occasionally
reached. I do not know what bearing my comment has
had, or my touchstones may have, upon the larger effects
of poetry or upon long poems. The long poem is partly
a different problem. I have of necessity confined both commentary and illustration to the slighter effects that seemed
to me commensurate with certain immediate qualities of
language. For, in the long run, whatever the poet's "philosophy," however wide may be the extension of his mean-

[1] Mr. F. O. Matthiessen informs me that my interpretation here, which
detaches the "yet" from the developing figure, is not the usual one. Mr.
Matthiessen refers the phrase to the gold, for which in his view it pre-
pares the way.

ing—like Milton's Ptolemaic universe in which he didn't believe—by his language shall you know him; the quality of his language is the valid limit of what he has to say.

I have not searched out the quotations that follow: they at once form the documentation and imply the personal bias from which this inquiry has grown. Only a few of the lines will be identified with the metaphysical technique, or, in Mr. Ransom's fine phrase, the metaphysical strategy. Strategy would here indicate the point on the intensive-extensive scale at which the poet deploys his resources of meaning. The metaphysical poet as a rationalist begins at or near the extensive or denoting end of the line; the romantic or Symbolist poet at the other, intensive end; and each by a straining feat of the imagination tries to push his meanings as far as he can towards the opposite end, so as to occupy the entire scale. I have offered one good and one bad example of the metaphysical strategy, but only defective examples of the Symbolist, which I cited as fallacies of mass language: Thomson was using language at its mass level, unhappily ignorant of the need to embody his connotations in a rational order of thought. (I allude here also, and in a quite literal sense, to Thomson's personal unhappiness, as well as to the excessive pessimism and excessive optimism of other poets of his time.) The great Symbolist poets, from Rimbaud to Yeats, have heeded this necessity of reason. It would be a hard task to choose between the two strategies, the Symbolist and the metaphysical; both at their best are great, and both are incomplete.

These touchstones, I believe, are not poetry of the extremes, but poetry of the center: poetry of tension, in which the "strategy" is diffused into the unitary effect.

Ask me no more whither doth hast
The Nightingale when May is past:
For in your sweet dividing throat
She winters, and keeps warm her note.

* * *

O thou Steeled Cognizance whose leap commits
The agile precincts of the lark's return . . .

* * *

That time of year thou mayst in me behold
When yellow leaves, or none, or few do hang
Upon those boughs which shake against the cold,
Bare ruined choirs where late the sweet birds sang.

* * *

Beauty is but a flower
Which wrinkles will devour;
Brightness falls from the air,
Queens have died young and fair,
Dust hath closed Helen's eye.
I am sick, I must die.
        Lord, have mercy upon us!

* * *

And then may chance thee to repent
The time that thou hast lost and spent

To cause thy lovers sigh and swoon;
Then shalt thou know beauty but lent,
And wish and want as I have done.

* * *

We have lingered in the chambers of the sea
By seagirls wreathed with seaweed red and brown
Till human voices wake us and we drown.

* * *

I am of Ireland
And the Holy Land of Ireland
And time runs on, cried she.
Come out of charity
And dance with me in Ireland.

* * *

And my poor fool is hanged! No, no, no life!
Why should a dog, a horse, a rat, have life
And thou no breath at all? Thou'lt come no more,
Never, never, never, never, never!—
Pray you undo this button; thank you, sir.—
Do you see this? Look on her,—look,—her lips,—
Look there, look there!

* * *

'Tis madness to resist or blame
The force of angry heavens flame:
And, if we would speak true,
Much to the Man is due,
Who, from his private Gardens, where
He liv'd reserved and austere,

> *As if his highest plot*
> *To plant the Bergamot,*
> *Could by industrious Valour climbe*
> *To ruin the great Work of Time,*
> *And cast the Kingdome old*
> *Into another Mold.*

*   *   *

Cover her face; mine eyes dazzle; she died young.

III

There are three more lines that I wish to look at: a tercet from the *Divine Comedy*. I know little of either Dante
or his language; yet I have chosen as my final instance of
tension—the instance itself will relieve me of the responsibility of the term—I have chosen not a great and difficult
passage, but only a slight and perfect one. It is from a scene
that has always been the delight of the amateur reader of
Dante; we can know more about it with less knowledge
than about any other, perhaps, in the poem. The damned
of the Second Circle are equivocally damned: Paolo and
Francesca were illicit lovers but their crime was incon-
tinence, neither adultery nor pandering, the two crimes of
sex for which Dante seems to find any real theological rep-
robation, for they are committed with the intent of injury.

You will remember that when Dante first sees the lovers
they are whirling in a high wind, the symbol here of lust.
When Francesca's conversation with the poet begins, the

wind dies down, and she tells him where she was born, in these lines:

> *Siede la terra dove nata fui*
> *Sulla marina dove il Po discende*
> *Per aver pace co' seguaci sui.*

Mr. Courtney Landon renders the tercet:

> *The town where I was born sits on the shore,*
> *Whither the Po descends to be at peace*
> *Together with the streams that follow him.*

But it misses a good deal; it misses the force of *seguaci* by rendering it as a verb. Professor Grandgent translates the third line: "To have peace with its pursuers," and comments: "The tributaries are conceived as chasing the Po down to the sea." Precisely; for if the *seguaci* are merely followers, not pursuers, the wonderfully ordered density of this simple passage is sacrificed. For although Francesca has told Dante where she lives, in the most directly descriptive language possible, she has told him more than that. Without the least imposition of strain upon the firmly denoted natural setting, she fuses herself with the river Po near which she was born. By a subtle shift of focus we see the pursued river as Francesca in Hell: the pursuing tributaries are a new visual image for the pursuing winds of lust. A further glance yields even more: as the winds, so the tributaries at once pursue and become one with the pursued; that is to say, Francesca has completely absorbed the substance of her sin—she is the sin; as, I believe it is said, the damned of the *Inferno* are plenary incarnations of the sin that has put them there. The tributaries of the Po are not only the winds of lust by analogy of visual images; they become identified by means of sound:

> ... *discende*
> *Per aver pace co' seguaci sui.*

The sibilants dominate the line; they are the hissing of the wind. But in the last line of the preceding tercet Francesca has been grateful that the wind has subsided so that she can be heard—

> *Mentre che il vento, come fa, si tace.*

After the wind has abated, then, we hear in the silence, for the first time, its hiss, in the susurration to the descending Po. The river is thus both a visual and an auditory image, and since Francesca is her sin and her sin is embodied in this image, we are entitled to say that it is a sin that we can both hear and see.

UNDERSTANDING
MODERN POETRY

About every six months I see in the *New York Times Book Review* the confident analogy between the audience of the modern poet and the audience that the English Romantics had to win in the early nineteenth century. Only wait a little while, and T. S. Eliot will be as easy for high-school teachers as "The Solitary Reaper." There may be some truth in this; but I think there is very little truth in it, and my reasons for thinking so will be the substance of this essay. There is a great deal of confusion about this matter, and not a little of it comes from the comfortable habit of citing a passage in the "Preface" to *Lyrical Ballads*, in which Wordsworth says that, as soon as the objects of modern life (meaning the physical changes wrought in society by the Industrial Revolution) become as familiar to the people as the old mythologies of poetry, the difficulties of apprehension and communication will disappear. But this has not happened. It is true that no modern poet has succeeded in knowing all the physical features of modern industrial society; but neither has "society" succeeded in this. It may be doubted that any poet in the past ever made a special point of studying the "techniques of production" of his time or of looking self-consciously at the objects around him as mere objects. Wordsworth himself did not.

Dante knew the science of the thirteenth century, and he was intensely aware of the physical features of his time —the ways of living, the clothing, the architecture, the implements of war, the natural landscape. But it was not a question of his becoming "familiar" with objects, though it cannot be denied that a relatively unchanging physical background, since it can be taken for granted, is an advantage to any poet. It is rather that *all* that he knew came under a philosophy which was at once dramatic myth, a body of truths, and a comprehensive view of life.

Now Wordsworth's point of view is still the point of view of the unreflecting reader, and it is a point of view appropriate and applicable to the poets of the Romantic movement who are still, to the general reader, all that poets ought to be or can be. But the modern poetry that our general reader finds baffling and obscure is a radical departure from the Romantic achievement; it contains features that his "education" has not prepared him for; neither in perception nor in intellect is he ready for a kind of poetry that does not offer him the familiar poetical objects alongside the familiar poetical truths.

Let us say, very briefly and only for the uses of this discussion, that the Romantic movement taught the reader to look for inherently poetical objects, and to respond to them "emotionally" in certain prescribed ways, these ways being indicated by the "truths" interjected at intervals among the poetical objects.

Certain modern poets offer no inherently poetical objects, and they fail to instruct the reader in the ways he must feel about the objects. All experience, then, becomes potentially the material of poetry—not merely the pretty and the agreeable—and the modern poet makes it possible for us to "respond" to this material in all the ways in which men everywhere may feel and think. On the ground of common sense—a criterion that the reader invokes against the eccentric moderns—the modern poet has a little the better of the argument, for to him poetry is not a special package tied up in pink ribbon: it is one of the ways that we have of knowing the world. And since the world is neither wholly pretty nor wholly easy to understand, poetry becomes a very difficult affair, demanding both in its writing and in its reading all the intellectual power that we have. But it is very hard for people to apply their minds to poetry, since it is one of our assumptions that come down from the early nineteenth century that our intellects are for mathematics and science, our emotions for poetry.

Who are these modern poets? Some twenty years ago they were supposed to be Mr. Lindsay, Mr. Masters, and Mr. Carl Sandburg. When Mr. Sandburg's poetry first appeared, it was said to be both ugly and obscure; now it is easy and beautiful to high-school students, and even to their teachers, whose more advanced age must have given them a prejudice in favor of the metrical, the pretty, and the "poetical" object. Doubtless the "obscure" moderns are the poets whom Mr. Max Eastman has ridiculed in *The Literary Mind,* and whom Mr. Cleanth Brooks, in *Modern Poetry and the Tradition,* distinguishes as the leaders of a poetic revolution as far-reaching as the Romantic revolution ushered in by *Lyrical Ballads* in 1798.

The volumes by Mr. Eastman and Mr. Brooks are of uneven value, but I recommend them to be read together; and I would suggest that it is exceedingly dangerous and misleading to read Mr. Eastman alone. Yet, although Mr. Eastman is aggressive, sensational, and personal in his attacks, he has been widely read; while Mr. Brooks, who is sober, restrained, and critical, will win one reader for Mr. Eastman's fifty. Mr. Eastman is a debater, not a critic; and he is plausible because, like the toothpaste manufacturer, he offers his product in the name of science. Reading his book some years ago, I expected on every page to see the picture of the white-coated doctor with the test tube and the goatee, and under it the caption: "Science says..." But why science? Simply because Mr. Eastman, being still in the Romantic movement, but not knowing that he is, insists that the poet get hold of some "truths" that will permit him to tell the reader what to think about the new poetical objects of our time: he must think scientifically or not at all. Eastman's *The Literary Mind* is an interesting document of our age; Brooks's *Modern Poetry and the Tradition* will probably survive as an epoch-making critical synthesis of the modern movement.

The poets of the new revolution range all the way from

the greatest distinction to charlatanism—a feature of every
revolution, literary or political. Mr. Eastman can make the
best moderns sound like the worst—as no doubt he could
make the great passages of "The Prelude" sound like
"Peter Bell" if he set his hand to it; and he found, as he
confesses with candor and chagrin, that certain passages in
the later works of Shakespeare strongly resemble some of
the poetry of the modern "Cult of Unintelligibility"; but
this hot potato, because he doesn't know what to do with
it, he quickly drops. It is not my purpose to make Mr.
Eastman the whipping-boy of a school of critics; of his
school, he is one of the best. What I wish to emphasize is
the negative of his somewhat sly contention that an admirer of Eliot's *Ash Wednesday* must also be an admirer
of Miss Stein's *Geography and Plays,* that there is only a
great lump of modernist verse in which no distinctions are
possible. By such tactics we could discredit Browning with
quotations from Mrs. Hemans. I notice this palpable non-
sense because Mr. Eastman has been widely read by professors of English, who are really rather glad to hear this
sort of thing, since it spares them the trouble of reading
a body of poetry for which there are no historical documents and of which generations of other professors have
not told them what to think.

In this essay I cannot elucidate a great many modern
poems—a task that at the present time would be only a
slight service to the reader; for in the state of his education
and mine, we should have to undertake the infinite series
of elucidations. We have no critical method; we have no

principles to guide us. Every poem being either a unique expression of personality or a response to an environment, we should know at the end of the tenth difficult poem only what we knew at the end of the first; we could only cite the personalities and the environments. What I wish to do here, then, is not to explain certain modern poems but rather to discuss the reasons, as I see them, why certain kinds of poetry are difficult today.

The most pervasive reason of all is the decline of the art of reading—in an age in which there is more print than the world has seen before. If you ask why this is so, the answer is that impressionistic education in all its varieties, chiefly the variety known as "progressive education," is rapidly making us a nation of illiterates: a nation of people without letters. For you do not have to attend to the letters and words on the page in order to "read" what is there. In an essay entitled "The Retreat of the Humanities" (*English Journal*, February, 1939, p. 127), Mr. Louis B. Wright quotes an interesting passage from another essay, "Supervising the Creative Teaching of Poetry," whose author Mr. Wright mercifully leaves anonymous:

The teaching of poetry divides itself naturally into two areas of enterprise, each with its essential conditioning validities.... Comprehending a poem need not involve any intellectual or formal concern with its technique, prose content, type, moral, diction, analysis, social implications, etc. Comprehending a poem is essentially an organic experience, essentially a response to the poetic stimulus of the author. Poetic comprehension may be verbalized or it may not.

In short, poetic comprehension does not involve anything at all, least of all the poem to be comprehended. Mr. Wright remarks that this is "equivalent to the emotion that comes from being tickled on the ear with a feather.... Before such ideas and such jargon, sincere advocates of learning sometimes retreat in despair." Yes; but for the sake of the good people whose "education" has doomed them to teach poetry with this monstrous jargon, I wish to examine the quotation more closely, and more in contempt than in despair. We have here, then, an offensive muddle of echoes ranging from business jargon through sociological jargon to the jargon of the Watsonian behaviorists. One must be more pleased than disappointed to find that poetry "naturally divides" itself, without any intellectual effort on our part, into "areas" having "conditioning validities" that are "essential"—an adjective that our Anonymity repeats twice adverbially in a wholly different non-sense. Now, if technique, diction, analysis, and the others are irrelevant in the reading of poetry, in what respect does poetry differ from automobiles: cannot one be conditioned to automobiles? No, that is not the answer. One is conditioned by responding to the "poetic stimulus of the author." One gets the poet's personality; and there's no use thinking about the poet's personality, since one cannot think, "verbalization" now being the substitute for thought—as indeed it is, in our Anonymity.

I am sure that thoughtful persons will have perceived, beyond this vulgar haze, an "idea" curiously resembling something that I have already said in this essay: it is astonishing how regularly the pseudo-scientific vocabularies are used in order to reach a poetic theory that the most ignorant "man in the street" already holds. That theory I call "decadent Romanticism," but I should like it to be plainly understood that I am not attacking the great Romantic poets. Romanticism gave us the "Ode to a Nightingale"; decadent Romanticism is now giving us the interminable ballads and local-color lyrics of Mr. Coffin and Mr. Stephen Benét—as it gave us, some twenty-five years ago, Joyce Kilmer's "Trees," which is indubitably the "favorite poem" of the American people, taught piously by every high-school teacher, and sometimes aggressively by college professors when they want to show what poetry ought to be; surely one of the preposterously bad lyrics in any language.

What I said earlier that I should like to call attention to again is: The weakness of the Romantic sensibility is that it gave us a poetry of "poetical" (or *poetized*) objects, pre-digested perceptions; and in case there should be any misunderstanding about the poetical nature of these objects, we also got "truths" attached to them—truths that in modern jargon are instructions to the reader to "respond" in a certain way to the poetical object, which is the "stimulus." And in the great body of nineteenth-century lyrical poetry —whose worst ancestor was verse of the type of Shelley's "I arise from dreams of thee"—the poet's personal emotions became the "poetic stimulus." The poem as a formal object to be looked at, to be studied, to be construed (in more than the grammatical sense, but first of all in that sense), dissolved into biography and history, so that in the long run the poetry was only a misunderstood pretext for the "study" of the sexual life of the poet, of the history of his age, of anything else that the scholar wished to "study"; and he usually wished to study anything but poetry.

Now our Anonymity has said that prose content, morals, and social implications are irrelevant in reading poetry, and it looks as if there were a fundamental disagreement between him and the biographical and historical scholars. There is no such disagreement. Once you arrive with Anonymity at the "poetic stimulus of the author," you have reached his biography and left his poetry behind; and, on principle, Anonymity cannot rule out the morals and the social implications (however much he may wish to rule them out), because morals and social implications are what you get when you discuss personality.

Before I proceed, I wish to enter a *caveat* to those persons who are thinking that I would dispense with historical scholarship. It is, in fact, indispensable; it is pernicious only when some ham actor in an English department uses it to wring tears from the Sophomores, by reciting the sad death of Percy Shelley. Let me illustrate one of its genuine uses. Here are the first two stanzas of Donne's "Valediction: forbidding mourning":

> *As virtous men passe mildly away,*
> *And whisper to their soules, to goe,*
> *Whilst some of their sad friends doe say,*
> *The breath goes now, and some say, no:*

> *Soe let us melt, and make no noise,*
> *No teare-floods, nor sigh-tempests move,*
> *T'were prophanation of our joyes*
> *To tell the layetie our love.*

The elaborate simile here asserts on several planes the analogy between the act of love and the moment of death. But if you happen to know that in Middle English and down through the sixteenth century the verb *die* has as a secondary meaning, "to perform the act of love," you are able to extend the analogy into a new frame of reference. The analogy contains a concealed pun. But we are detecting the pun not in order to show that a man in the late sixteenth century was still aware of the early, secondary meaning of *die;* we are simply using this piece of information to extend our knowledge of what happens in the first eight lines of the poem. It is of no interest to anybody that Donne knew how to make this pun; it is of capital interest to know what the pun does to the meaning of the poem.

I have seemed to be talking about what I consider bad poetic theory; but I have also been talking about something much larger, that cannot here be adequately discussed: I have been talking about a bad theory of education. If only briefly, I must notice it because it abets the bad poetic theory and is at the bottom of the popular complaint that modern poetry is difficult. The complainant assumes that he understands all English poetry up to, say, about 1917—a date that I select because in that year Eliot's *Prufrock and Other Poems* was published. But, as a matter of fact, the complainant does not understand Marvel and Donne any better than he understands Eliot; and I doubt if he can read Sydney any better than he can read Pound; he could not read Raleigh at all, and he has never heard of Fulke Greville.

So it is not "modern" poetry which is difficult; it is rather a certain kind of poetry as old, in English, as the sixteenth century, and, in Italian, much older than that. It is a kind of poetry that requires of the reader the fullest co-operation of all his intellectual resources, all his knowledge of the world, and all the persistence and alertness that he now thinks only of giving to scientific studies.

This kind of poetry must have the direct and *active* participation of a reader who today, because he has been pampered by bad education, expects to lie down and be *passive* when he is reading poetry. He admits, for some obscure reason, that poetry is a part of his education; but he has been taught to believe that education is *conditioning*: something is being done to him, he is not doing anything himself. And that is why he cannot read poetry.

A conditioning theory of education may be good enough for animals in the zoo, but it is not good enough for human beings; and it is time that this symptom of decadence were known for what it is, and not as enlightenment, "science," liberalism, and democracy. I do not know whether we are living in a democracy; it is, at any rate, an anomaly of democratic theory that it should produce, in education, a theory that we are bundles of reflexes without intelligence.

The theory assumes, first of all, that education is a process of getting adjusted to an environment. Something known as "personality" is making *responses* to things known as *stimuli*. In the educational environment there are *stimuli* called "poems," to which you make responses.

Now while you are making a response, you are not doing more than a chimpanzee or a Yahoo would be doing. But should you do more than respond, you might perform an act of intelligence, of knowing, of cognition. In the conditioning theory there is no cognition because there is no intelligence. Of what use is intelligence? It does not at all help to describe the "behavior" of persons who are getting responses from the *stimuli* of poems. What the poem is in itself, what it says, is no matter. It is an irrelevant question. But if you can imagine it not to be irrelevant, if you can imagine "Lycidas" to be something else than the stimulation of "drives," "appetites," "attitudes," in certain "areas," then you have got to use your intelligence, which, after you have been progressively educated, you probably no longer have.

As I conceive this gloomy situation, it is far more complicated than the violent synopsis of it that I have just sketched. The complications would distribute the blame to many historical villains, of whom the teachers-college racketeers (some of them misguided idealists) are only a conspicuous contemporary group. The trouble goes far back, farther even than the Romantic movement, when, for the first time in Western art, we had the belief that poetry is chiefly or even wholly an emotional experience.

Does poetry give us an emotional experience? What is an "emotional experience"? And what is an "intellectual experience"?

These are difficult questions. We are proceeding today as if they were no longer questions, as if we knew the answers, and knew them as incontestable truths. If by "an emotional experience" we mean one in which we find ourselves "moved," then we mean nothing; we are only translating a Latin word into English: a tautology. If by "an intellectual experience" we mean that we are using our minds on the relations of words, the relation of words and rhythm, the relation of the abstract words to the images, all the relations together—and if, moreover, we succeed in reducing all these things to the complete determination of logic, so that there is nothing left over, then this intellectual experience is a tautology similar to that of the emotional experience: we are intellectually using our intellects, as before we were emotionally being moved. But if on the other hand, as in the great seventeenth-century poets, you find that exhaustive analysis applied to the texture of image and metaphor fails to turn up any inconsistency, and at the same time fails to get all the meaning of the poem into a logical statement, you are participating in a poetic experience. And both intellect and emotion become meaningless in discussing it.

I have had to make that statement abstract, or not at all; it needs many pages of illustration. I can cite only three examples of poetry, which I hope will somewhat illuminate it. The first example is William Browne's slight "Epitaph on the Countesse Dowager of Pembroke," a favorite anthology piece, and one that is neither in the metaphysical style of its period nor romantically modern:

> *Underneath this sable Herse*
> *Lyes the subject of all verse:*
> *Sydney's sister, Pembroke's Mother:*
> *Death, ere thou hast slaine another*
> *Faire and learned and good as she,*
> *Time shall throw a dart at thee.*

I find this poem perennially moving (exciting, interesting), and it is plain that we cannot be moved by it until we understand it; and to understand it we have got to *analyze* the meaning of the difference here asserted as existing between Time and Death, who are dramatically personified and in conflict. Since, in one of the major modes of poetry, Death is conceived as the work of Time, we must perform a dissociation of ideas, and see Time as turning against himself, so that the destruction of Death is actually the destruction of Time. However far you may take these distinctions, no inconsistency appears; nothing contradicts anything else that is said in the poem; yet we have not reduced the poem to strict logic. Browne has offered certain particulars that are irreducible: the Sydney and Pembroke families (for the sake of whose dignity this upheaval of the order of nature will occur); and then there is the dart, a dramatic and particular image that does not contradict, yet cannot be assimilated into, a logical paraphrase of the poem. Is this poem an emotional experience? And yet it is not an "intellectual" experience.

The second quotation must be slighted, but it is so familiar that a few lines will bring the whole poem before the reader—Shelley's "When the lamp is shattered"; I quote the last stanza:

> *Its [Love's] passions will rock thee,*
> *As the storms rock the ravens on high:*
> *Bright reason will mock thee,*
> *Like the sun from a wintry sky.*
> *From thy nest every rafter*
> *Will rot, and thine eagle home*
> *Leave thee naked to laughter,*
> *When leaves fall and cold winds come.*

The general "argument" is that the passing of spiritual communion from lovers leaves them sad and, in this last stanza, the prey of lust and self-mockery, and even of the mockery of the world ("naked to laughter"). The first line sets the tone and the "response" that the reader is to maintain to the end: we are told in advance what the following lines will mean: an abstraction that will relieve us of the trouble of examining the particular instances. Indeed, when these appear, the development of their imagery is confused and vague. The ravens in the second line are eagles in the sixth; but, after all, they are only generically birds; greater particularity in them would have compromised their poeticism as objects, or interfered with the response we are instructed to make to them. I pass over

"Bright reason," the self-mockery, for the mockery of the world. Are we to suppose that other birds come by and mock the raven (eagle), or are we to shift the field of imagery and see "thee" as a woman? Now in the finest poetry we cannot have it both ways. We can have a multiple meaning through ambiguity, but we cannot have an incoherent structure of images. Shelley, in confusion, or carelessness, or haste, could not sustain the nest-bird metaphor and say all that he wished to say; so, in order to say it, he changed the figure and ruined the poem. The more we track down the implications of his imagery, the greater the confusion; the more we track down the implications of the imagery in the best verse of Donne, Marvel, Raleigh, Milton, Hopkins, Yeats, Eliot, Ransom, Stevens, the richer the meaning of the poem. Shelley's poem is confused. Are we to conclude that therefore it offers an emotional experience?

In conclusion, one more poem—this one by W. H. Auden:

> Our hunting fathers told the story
> Of the sadness of the creatures,
> Pitied the limits and the lack
> Set in their finished features;
> Saw in the lion's intolerant look,
> Behind the quarry's dying glare
> Love raging for the personal glory
> That reason's gift would add,
> The liberal appetite and power,
> The rightness of a god.

Who nurtured in that fine tradition
Predicted the result,
Guessed love by nature suited to
The intricate ways of guilt;
That human company could so
His southern gestures modify
And make it his mature ambition
To think no thought but ours,
To hunger, work illegally,
And be anonymous?

In this poem there is an immense complication of metaphor, but I do not propose to unravel it. I would say just this: that all the complications can be returned without confusion or contradiction to a definite, literal, and coherent field of imagery; that when the poet wishes to extend his meaning, he does it by means of this field of metaphor, not by changing the figure, which is: the hunter debases his human nature (Love) in his arrogant, predatory conquest of the world, and Love itself becomes not merely morally bad but evil. The field of imagery, to which all the implications refer, is that of the hunting squire, who by a deft ambiguity quickly becomes predatory man.

I halt the analysis here because, as I have already said, we need something more fundamental in reading poetry than the occasional analyses of poems. I would say then, in conclusion, that modern poetry is difficult because we have lost the art of reading any poetry that will not read itself to us; that thus our trouble is a fundamental problem of education, which may be more fundamental than education. We may be approaching the time when we shall no longer be able to read anything and shall be subject to passive conditioning. Until this shall happen, however, we might possibly begin to look upon language as a field of study, not as an impressionistic debauch. If we wish to understand anything, there is only the hard way; if we wish to understand Donne and Eliot, perhaps we had better begin, young, to read the classical languages, and a little later the philosophers. There is probably no other way.

MISS EMILY AND THE
BIBLIOGRAPHER[1]

THE SCENE is a seminar room at a large American university. It is the first meeting of the year. The eager young man asks the professor a question. "What," he says, "is the ultimate purpose of graduate research in English literature?" The professor, whose special field is English bibliography of the decade 1840-1850, does not hesitate. "To lay the foundations of literary criticism," he replies. The eager young man is pleased because secretly and discreetly he hopes that some day he may hope to be a critic. A month later the bibliographer assigns the group a paper. "Gentlemen," he says, "we must maintain in these papers the graduate point of view. There must be no impressionism. There must be no literary criticism. Anybody can write that."

I came upon this tale about a year ago but a year before that I had read one like it in an essay written by Mr. John Crowe Ransom some time before the incident that I relate occurred. I began to wonder if Mr. Ransom had made it up; then I began to hope that he had, so that the witnessed

[1] This paper was read before the English Club of Princeton University, April 10, 1940.

100

fact should stand as proof of an insight. Without the witnessed fact Mr. Ransom (I assume for my purpose that he
invented the tale) would be in the position of William
Faulkner after his story, "A Rose for Emily," appeared.
You will remember Mr. Faulkner's story. Miss Emily, a
curious spinster, conceals the dead body of her lover in
an upstairs bedroom until concealment is no longer possible. Nobody believed this tale; it was one of Mr. Faulkner's outrageous lies; it just couldn't have happened. Then
it happened. This evidence of the decadence of the South
emerged about three years later from a farmhouse in up-
state New York. A middle-aged woman had killed her
lover and kept the body.

For both Mr. Ransom and Mr. Faulkner the later facts
confirmed the previous insights. Yet I must confess that
for another reason altogether the analogy teases my fancy.
Both tales are tales of horror, and I submit that the greater
horror, for me, is in the scholar's insincerity. The analogy,
like a good one, holds on more than one level. Must we
not suspect that Miss Emily had a time of it conducting
her intrigue in a provincial American community and
that she probably, with the lover's last breath, breathed
her sigh of relief? The need of judging him as a living
man had been happily removed with the removal of his
breath; the contingencies of personality were happily gone;
she could have him without any of the social dangers of
having him. She could now proceed without interruption
to the reconstruction of the history of her love. But there
was always the body, and the body wrecks the analogy.

Miss Emily's historical method recognized that it was the history of something it could not ignore and had to return to. But the specialist in English bibliography of the decade 1840-1850 would doubtless bury the body at once, concealing it forever; and he would never afterwards have to be reminded what he was doing the bibliography of. Or if you will give° this figure yet another turn, the analogy is wrecked again, again in favor of Miss Emily. The body has got to decompose, and its existence will become shockingly known—a crisis that the historical scholars conspire among themselves to postpone indefinitely; and if the wild discourtesy of the real world reminds them of it they say, "No, you are mistaken; we buried it long ago." But have they? Can they? And that is why Miss Emily remains a somewhat endearing horror for me. It is better to pretend with Miss Emily that something dead is living than to pretend with the bibliographer that something living is dead.

The bibliographer's belief that "anybody can write that" I wish to discuss later, when I get to some of the more dialectical phases of the question. Here I should like to set off against my frivolity what many literary critics have called the insincerity of the academic mind. Between the frivolity and the insincerity, between the ignorance and the irrelevant learning, the outlook for a literary criticism in our time is dark. But as a matter of fact, whatever may be said of the party of ignorance, it would be hard to maintain that anything like personal insincerity motivates the activities of the historical scholars. Every point of view entails upon its proponents its own kind of insincerity. Yet the evidence for the insincerity of our bibliographer is damaging: what, if not insincerity, lies back of his professed purpose which he, at the first showdown, shamelessly repudiates? How can he spend years laying the foundations of literary criticism when he thinks that anybody can write it? If anybody can write it does it need the collaboration of many generations of scholarship to lay its foundations?

There is insincerity here no doubt; for it is plainly an instance of a professed intention that one never expects to carry out or that one vaguely expects the future to perform for us. Does this not have an ominous and familiar sound? We hear it in the world at large and on nearly every level of our experience.

We hear it in politics, and the political voice has its counterpoint in the uneasy speculation of the journalist critics about the future of literature: some ten years ago we got from England a whole series of little books called *The Future of—*; and it is seldom that we get an essay on the present state of letters or even on a single book that does not look far beyond the occasion. We are asked as citizens to live only for the future, either in the preservation of democracy or in the creation of the classless society. Mr. T. S. Eliot has discussed this question in "Literature and the Modern World," an essay which I believe has not been reprinted in any of his books; he examines the point of view of H. G. Wells and sees in it the widespread eschatology of a secular, naturalistic philosophy. As individuals today we must subordinate our spiritual life and our material satisfactions to the single purpose of gaining superior material satisfactions in the future, which will be a naturalistic Utopia of mindless hygiene and Tom Swift's gadgets. There is no doubt that the most powerful attraction offered us by the totalitarian political philosophies is the promise of irresponsible perfection in the future, to be gained at the slight cost of our present consent to extinguish our moral natures in a group mind.

The moral nature affirms itself in judgment, and we cannot or will not judge. Because the scholars as much as other people today are involved in the naturalistic temper, they also refuse to judge. The historical scholar says that we cannot judge the literature of our time because we do not know whether the future will approve of it. Is he not obviously evading his moral responsibility? I do not say he evades it as a father or as a citizen; but he does evade it in the specific field in which he ought to exercise it, since of that field he professes knowledge.

He has reasons for the Great Refusal, and the reasons are of curious interest and at the same time of critical importance. In order to express my sense of their significance I must go a long way round. I should like to begin by citing certain critical views held by Mr. Edmund Wilson, a brilliant historian of literature, who because he puts literature above research may be expected to exhibit some of the values of the historical method when it is actually applied in criticism.

Let me first make a distinction—so broad that if it is good it will be virtually a truism. Let us assume that English critics from the late Renaissance to Coleridge had a firm sense of the differences among the *genres* of literature and that they tried constantly to state those differences critically. Whether they succeeded in this task, from our point of view, is not the question; it is rather that they tried to look upon works of literature as objective existences with respect to the different forms.

Taking up this defeated tradition we still from time to time consider the relation of poetry to prose fiction. Our approach to this problem was adumbrated by Coleridge in a fashion that would have been unintelligible a century before his time: in Chapter XIV of *Biographia Literaria* he remarks that a work of prose fiction will often have the imaginative qualities of poetry, no essential difference between poetry and fiction being discernible.[2] There are concealed in this view certain metaphysical assumptions, which we still use without awareness of the metaphysics. (In the study of "English" we are forbidden to "use" philosophy—which means that we are using it badly.) We say today that there is poetry in prose fiction and, wherever you have narrative, fiction in poetry. But it ought to be easy to see that the murk enveloping the question when we try to carry it further than this arises from a certain kind of fallacy of abstraction. We are thinking in terms of substance, or essence. Those who believe that poetry and prose fiction differ in some fundamental sense assume that poetry is a distinct essence; whether prose has an essence is irrelevant since it could not have the essence

[2] For a more detailed discussion of this problem see pp. 45 ff.

of poetry; and therefore, prose fiction being a kind of prose, it is essentially different from poetry.

Now Mr. Wilson easily disposes of this argument in a famous essay called "Is Verse a Dying Technique?" (by which I understand him to mean: Is verse becoming an unpopular technique?). He boldly denies to poetry an essence distinct from the essence of prose. In denying a difference he affirms the same essence of both: he thinks in terms of essence. He shows that *Madame Bovary* contains a great deal of "poetry" and concludes that the only interesting difference between a work like Flaubert's masterpiece and the *Aeneid* is that the one is in prose, the other in verse. That is certainly a difference; it is according to Mr. Wilson strictly a difference of "technique"; and he assumes the likenesses in terms of a common essence. Here we get the deepest assumption of the literary historian: the subject matter alone has objective status, the specific form of the work being external and mechanical—mere technique. This large essence common to all literature is human life. Both Flaubert and Virgil were concerned with it in its largest implications.

Nobody will deny this; but it is critically irrelevant to affirm it. Within the terms of this affirmation critical thought is impossible, and we succumb to the documentary routine which "correlates" this de-formed substance with its origin, which by convention is called history.

Now the writers who see in works of literature not the specific formal properties but only the amount and range of human life brought to the reader are expressionists.

Back of the many varieties of expressionist theory lies the assumption of the common or the distinct essence. If I say that the essence of *Madame Bovary* is different from the essence of the *Aeneid* and Mr. Wilson says that the essences are the same, we merely shout our opinions at each other, and the louder voice prevails. The historical method will not permit us to develop a critical instrument for dealing with works of literature as existent objects; we see them as expressive of substances beyond themselves. At the historical level the work expresses its place and time, or the author's personality, but if the scholar goes further and says anything about the work, he is expressing himself. Expressionism is here a sentiment, forbidding us to think and permitting us to feel as we please. When the bored expressionist tires of the pure artistic essence he turns into the inquisitive literary historian; or he may be both at once, as indeed he often is.

The great historical scholars of our time are notoriously deficient critics, but critics they are nevertheless. I am far from believing that the bibliographer's defense of scholarship is acceptable to all the scholars, many of whom are certain that they are already doing for criticism all that is necessary. Do you want a critic? Why, we already have one—in John Livingston Lowes. Has he not given us *Convention and Revolt*? Yes, he has; but in the course of a few pages I cannot do justice to the historical scholarship that gave us the facile seesaw picture of the history of poetry, or to the poetic learning that permitted Mr. Lowes to take seriously the late Amy Lowell. The mere literary critics took Miss Lowell seriously for a while, but the literary critics were not scholars. If you will think of *Convention and Revolt* along with *The Road to Xanadu* you will see that the literary dilettante and the historical scholar can flourish, without much communication between them, in one man.

Do we not encounter here one of the remarkable insights of the late Irving Babbitt? His *Literature and the American College,* published in 1908, is still quoted, but there is no reason to believe its message has ever been taken seriously by the men who most need it. At that time the late J. E. Spingarn had not imported into American criticism the term expressionism. Mr. Babbitt called the dilettantes Rousseauistic impressionists; the historical scholars Baconian naturalists. Both dilettante and scholar repudiated the obligations of judgment because both alike were victims of a naturalistic philosophy. I believe Mr. Babbitt did not consider the possibility of their being the same man. He saw on the one hand the ignorant journalist critics, "decadent romantics," for whom intensity of feeling was the sole critical standard; and on the other hand the historical scholars, who had no critical standard at all but who amassed irrelevant information. It was—and still is—a situation in which it is virtually impossible for a young man to get a critical, literary education. If he goes to a graduate school he comes out incapacitated for criticism; if he tries to be a critic he is not unlike the ignorant impressionist who did not go to the graduate school. He cannot discuss the literary object in terms of its specific form; all that he can do is to give you its history or tell you how he feels about it. The concrete form of the play, the poem, the novel, that gave rise to the history or the feeling lies neglected on the hither side of the Styx, where Virgil explains to Dante that it is scorned alike by heaven and hell.

Mr. Babbitt saw in the aesthete and the historical scholar the same motivation. The naturalism of the scholar lies in his mechanical theory of history, a theory in which the literary object is dissolved into the determinism of forces surrounding it. The naturalism of the aesthete operates on the psychological plane; he responds to the aesthetic object in terms of sensation and if the sensation is intense the aesthetic object is good.

Mr. Babbitt scolded these erring brothers for not making a moral judgment, and it is just here that the limitations of his method appear. The moral obligation to judge does not necessarily obligate us to make a moral judgment. Mr. Babbitt's humanism contains some concealed naturalism in its insistence upon the value of the mere substance or essence of literature: the subject matter itself must be decorous in order to pass the humanist examination. The specific property of a work of literary art which differentiates it from mere historical experience he could never understand; and it is this specific property, this particular quality of the work, that puts upon us the moral obligation to form a judgment. Mr. Yvor Winters remarks that Mr. Babbitt never understood "how the moral intelligence gets into poetry." It gets in not as moral abstractions but as form, coherence of image and metaphor, control of tone and of rhythm, the union of these features. So the moral obligation to judge compels us to make not a moral but a relevant judgment.

The question in the end comes down to this: What as literary critics are we to judge? As literary critics we must first of all decide in what respect the literary work has a specific objectivity. If we deny its specific objectivity then not only is criticism impossible but literature also. We have got to decide what it is about the whole of a work of literature which distinguishes it from its parts—or rather the parts we can abstract from this whole and then distribute over the vast smudge of history, whence they presumably were derived. It is just a question of knowing before we talk what as critics we are talking about.

From my point of view the formal qualities of a poem are the focus of the specifically critical judgment because they partake of an objectivity that the subject matter, abstracted from the form, wholly lacks. The form of "Lycidas" is Milton's specific achievement as a poet in the convention of the pastoral elegy; but this convention, which is his substance, represents in itself only a subjective selection from Milton's historical situation. Would it not be simpler to seize at once the specific quality of "Lycidas" and try to understand it than to grapple with that aspect which fades into the immense perspective of history?

It would be simpler, if not easier, to discuss the form if we had a way of discussing it; yet before we can understand a literary problem we must first confess the problem exists. We no longer admit the problem because we no longer believe in the specific quality of the work of literature, the quality that distinguishes it from a work of history or even of science. As men of letters we no longer, in fact, believe in literature; we believe rather that the knowledge offered us in even the most highly developed literary forms has something factitious and illusory about it, so that before we can begin to test its validity we must translate it into an analogy derived from the sciences. The historical method is an imitation of scientific method: we entertain as interesting and valuable that portion of the literary work to which we can apply the scientific vocabularies.

Not being a literary historian I do not know when the literary profession lost confidence in literature; I suppose it was a gradual loss; we see its beginnings in the English romantics, and we do not yet see the end. The rise of the sciences, their immense practical successes, even their moral failures, intimidated the scholars and I seem to hear them say, at first secretly and late at night when black questions cannot be gainsaid: "Milton's science is false, and the scientists say that his moral and religious ideas have no empirical validity. But if I give up Milton I give up my profession, so I had better bestir myself to study scientifically Milton's unscientific science. We must get in on the wonderful scientific triumphs of the age. Nobody believes today that the arts give us a sort of cognition at least equally valid with that of scientific method; so we will just take the arts as fields of data for more scientific investigation."

The historical method is in the long run the unhistorical method. The literary historians are not first of all historians. We seldom get from them anything like Taine on English literature; no American English scholar has produced a work of the distinction of Carl Becker's *The Heavenly City of the Eighteenth Century Philosophers,* a book written not in the historical method but out of the historical imagination. It is a work of literature by a mind informed with a mature point of view and seasoned with exact knowledge (by knowledge I do not mean documentation) in many fields. Could Mr. Becker have written the book had he been trained in the belief that philosophy, for example, not being "English," has no place in historical writing? Could he have written it had he been compelled to suppress all the resources of his intelligence but the single one employed in the mechanical "correlation" of literature with the undigested lump of history? Is there not an instructive moral in the distinction of Mr. Becker's prose style?

I am not attacking the study or the writing of history for use in the criticism of literature. I am attacking the historical method. I trust everybody understands what this method is. It reflects at varying distances the philosophies of monism current in the nineteenth century and still prevailing today. Because the literary scholar in his monistic naturalism cannot discern the objectivity of the forms of literature, he can only apply to literature certain abstractions which he derives, two stages removed, from the naturalistic sciences; that is to say he gets these abstractions from the historians who got them from the scientists. In the period when physics was the popular science we got historical studies of influences, conceived in terms of forces, causes, and effects; then came the biological analogies that gave us organic periods where we attended to growths and developments; and today we have a broadening of the historical method which reflects the vast extension of scientific procedure in the semi-sciences—psychology, economics, and sociology.

That this method is, in a definite sense, unhistorical it would not be hard to show. Under whatever leading analogy we employ the historical method—organism, mechanism, causality—it has the immediate effect of removing the historian himself from history, so that he cannot participate as a living imagination in a great work of literature. Even those scholars, usually men interested in the eighteenth century, who are concerned with the meaning of tradition conceive of tradition itself in terms of scientific analogies, so that there is something remote and mechanical about a tradition; and the tradition that we are interested in is almost always seen as a traditional "body" of literature, not operative today—not living, as the very word body implies.

This removal of the historian from living history has curious consequences. Because it is difficult—or too easy in some respects—to get historical documents for works of the present or recent past we refuse to study them. And we also refuse to study them because their reputations are not fixed. There is here the assumption, as I think the illusion, that the reputation of any writer is ever fixed. These two illusions—the necessity of documents for the study of literature and the fixed hierarchy of the past—are not necessarily consequences of the historical method: Milton complained of similar routines of pedantry at Cambridge. Yet perhaps more today than ever we get a systematic, semi-philosophical sanction for our refusal to study literature.

I take the somewhat naïve view that the literature of the past began somewhere a few minutes ago and that the literature of the present begins, say, with Homer. While there is no doubt that we need as much knowledge of all kinds, from all sources, as we can get if we are to see the slightest lyric in all its richness of meaning, we have nevertheless an obligation, that we perilously evade, to form a judgment of the literature of our own time. It is more than an obligation; we must do it if we would keep on living. When the scholar assumes that he is judging a work of the past from a high and disinterested position he is actually judging it from no position at all but is only abstracting from the work those qualities that his semiscientific method will permit him to see; and this is the Great Refusal.

We must judge the past and keep it alive by being alive ourselves; and that is to say that we must judge the past not with a method or an abstract hierarchy but with the present, or with as much of the present as our poets have

succeeded in elevating to the objectivity of form. For it is
through the formed, objective experience of our own time
that we must approach the past; and then by means of a
critical mastery of our own formed experience we may test
the presence and the value of form in works of the past.
This critical activity is reciprocal and simultaneous. The
scholar who tells us that he understands Dryden but makes
nothing of Hopkins or Yeats is telling us that he does not
understand Dryden.

Perhaps the same scholar acknowledges the greatness of
Dryden and the even more formidable greatness of Milton
and Shakespeare; and if you ask him how they became
great he will reply, as I have heard him reply, that History
did it and that we have got to wait until History does it,
or declines to do it, to writers of our own time. Who is
this mysterious person named History? We are back again
with our old friend, the Great Refusal, who thrives upon
the naturalistic repudiation of the moral obligation to
judge. If we wait for history to judge there will be no
judgment; for if we are not history then history is nobody.
He is nobody when he has become the historical method.

One last feature of this illusion of the fixed hierarchy
I confess I cannot understand. It is the curious belief that
the chief function of criticism is the ranking of authors
rather than their use. It is the assumption that the great
writers of the past occupy a fixed position. If we alter
the figure slightly, admitting that History has frozen their
reputations, we must assume also that the position from
which we look at them is likewise fixed; for if it were

not we should see them in constantly changing relations and perspectives, and we should think their positions were changing too. If you will now see this same figure as a landscape of hills, trees, plains, you will quickly become fearful for the man who from a fixed point surveys the unchanging scene; for the man, the only man, who cannot change his position is a dead man: the only man for whom the greatness of the great poets is fixed is also dead. And so, if we may look at this Homeric simile with the eyes of Bishop Berkeley, we must conclude that the great authors are dead too, because there is nobody to look at them. I have adapted this figure from one of the Prefaces of Henry James because it seems to me to be a good way of saying that the literature of the past can be kept alive only by seeing it as the literature of the present. Or perhaps we ought to say that the literature of the past lives in the literature of the present and nowhere else; that it is all present literature.

HARDY'S PHILOSOPHIC
METAPHORS

I

AFTER THOMAS HARDY had become a great literary figure on the British model—that is to say, a personage
to whom one makes pilgrimages—criticism of his works
languished: once the battle over the obscenity of Jude and
the pessimism of his "philosophy" had been won, nobody
had very much to say, except that one admired him. So
far as I know, only two critical works on Hardy exist:
Lionel Johnson's fine study of the novels, *The Art of
Thomas Hardy,* which, first published in 1894, appeared
before Hardy was known as a poet; and Lascelles Aber-
crombie's *Thomas Hardy,* a book of considerable value for
the criticism of the novels but of not much use for the
poetry. One must add to these works the excellent essay,
"The Poetry of Thomas Hardy," by J. E. Barton, which
appears as an appendix to the John Lane edition of Johnson's book (1923). The centennial biography, *Hardy of
Wessex,* by C. J. Weber, no doubt adds to our store of
facts about Hardy; yet Mr. Weber's critical ineptitude
contributes little to our understanding of either the poetry
or the novels.

For two reasons I have wished to make this comment upon the critics of Hardy's poetry: they have given us very little to start with, and their assertion of Hardy's greatness as a poet is worse than nothing to start with. I do not intend in this commentary to deny the "greatness" of Hardy's poetry, nor to deny meaning to the pious enthusiasm of two generations of devoted readers, among whom intermittently I count myself. But I do think at the same time that the enthusiasm is partly sentimental; it implies an equivocal judgment of both the poetry and the man. It is sentimental because it does not distinguish man from poet or tell us upon what terms we may talk about them together. We have here in the case of Hardy—though for no doubt quite different reasons—the figure of the poet-sage not unlike that of Mr. Robert Frost, whose admirers will not permit the critics to dissociate the poetry from the wise man who wrote it. When without the admirers' permission a critic like Mr. R. P. Blackmur assumes that his task is to discuss Mr. Frost's language, he suffers the fanatical obloquy of a popular spellbinder, Mr. Bernard DeVoto, who promptly calls Mr. Blackmur a fool.

Now very much the same sort of thing went on towards the end of Thomas Hardy's life, and one must suspect very strongly, from all the evidence, that he liked it, and that he liked it because, like most critically naïve minds, he could accept the personal tribute as tribute to the power of his message, which was the message of a "philosopher." Hardy was a great poet, but I arrive at that conclusion after disposing of a strong prejudice against the personal qualities that have led his admirers to believe him a great man. I see him as a somewhat complacent and tiresome old gentleman, mellow and wise; a man who in his youth had set about conquering a career; who married a woman his inferior but above him socially, and could never forget the social difference—a fact that forbids us to forget it; who permitted his literary reputation to lead him into the tow of society hostesses who could have seen in him only his fame and from whom, as he frequently confessed, he got nothing. Yet he continued until late in life to appear as the literary lion. Why did he do it? It is useless to pretend that Thomas Hardy's social sense was distinguished (a distinction that has nothing to do with "class") or that he was not lacking in a certain knowledge of the world that would have been valuable even to the historian of a yeoman society: in so far as historical and biographical criticism will illuminate Hardy's poetry, it is important to keep his defects steadily in mind, for he never overcame them. Shakespeare's origins were humbler than Hardy's, yet they are irrelevant in the criticism of Shakespeare, because the confusion of feeling that one finds in Hardy cannot be found in Shakespeare. Hardy's background and education, like other backgrounds and other educations for poetry, will give us a clew to the defects of the work, but not to its merits, and it is with the merits that criticism must be specifically occupied. Literature can be written from any background, and Hardy wrote literature.

Mr. Weber quotes from Hardy's famous description of Clym Yeobright the following passage, and applies it to Hardy's own young manhood:

Mentally he was in a provincial future, that is, he was in many points abreast with the central town thinkers of his date. Much of this development he may have owed to his studious life in Paris, where he had become acquainted with ethical systems popular at the time. In consequence of this relatively advanced position, Yeobright might have been called unfortunate. The rural world was not ripe for him.

From this and other passages in the novels, in which Hardy presents himself in the disguise of certain characters, we get a portrait of the young Hardy against the background from which he sprang. Like Yeobright he was a young man "educated" out of the folk culture of his region: he had read Darwin, Huxley, Hume, Gibbon—the Victorian agnostics and their naturalistic forerunners of the eighteenth century. He began to see the world through "ethical systems popular at the time"; more than that, he began to see the people of Dorset in terms of the metaphysical bias of these systems; so that when he came back to Dorset from his studies in London he must have felt that his "advanced position" had cut him off from his people.

Yet there can be no doubt that, if this situation actually confronted Hardy at the outset of his literary career, it offered him tremendous advantages. He had been possessed from birth of an immense, almost instinctive knowledge of the life of a people rooted in ancient folk-traditions and fixed, also, in the objective patterns of nature and of the occupations close to nature. This knowledge of a provincial scene, where "life had bared its bones" to him, must have toughened his skepticism against the cruder aspects of Victorian thought, liberalism, optimism, and the doctrine of progress, and he could concentrate with a sort of classical purity upon the permanent human experiences.

Yet he did have a philosophical view of the significance of the human situation. As William R. Rutland indicates in his *Thomas Hardy* (the best general book on the subject), Hardy maintained with great consistency, from the beginning of his literary career, a philosophical attitude. The attitude did not change. Mr. Rutland makes an astute analysis of it:

It is an interesting paradox that Hardy should have placed so high a value upon intellectual reason, while his own mental life was almost entirely governed by emotion . . . he criticized J. H. Newman for failing to provide logical support for his beliefs. The outlook upon life of his mature manhood was almost wholly due to emotional reactions against suffering and injustice; but he sought for intellectual explanations of the universe in the writing of the philosophers. He went on reading philosophy till he was old, but he never advanced beyond what had been in the forefront of thought during his early manhood. When, in 1915, he read that no modern philosopher subscribes to Herbert Spencer's doctrine of "the Unknowable" (which had greatly influenced him) he declared himself "utterly bewildered."

How much this philosophical reading did towards making the young Hardy, like Clym Yeobright, an outsider in his own region, nobody could calculate accurately; but that it did affect him in this manner I believe no one will deny. His "advanced position" is only another way of saying that he had very early come to be both inside and outside his background, which was to be the material of his art: an ambivalent point of view that, in its infinite variations from any formula that we may state for it, is at the center of the ironic consciousness. While Hardy had a direct "emotional reaction" to his Wessex people, who were the human substance of the only world he really knew, he nevertheless tried to philosophize about them in the terms of Victorian materialism.

This, I think, was his intellectual situation, and Mr. Rutland has given us a clew to its meaning that ought to receive at some future time a more detailed analysis than I can give it here. In setting forth the experiences of people deeply involved with the cycle of the earth and "conditioned" in their emotional relations by close familiarity with the processes of nature, he had constantly before him a kind of "naturalism" that only an astute philosophical mind could have kept, in that period, distinct from a naturalism of a wholly different order: the philosophic naturalism of Huxley and Spencer which, according to Mr. Rutland, Hardy tended to look upon as "explanations" of the world, not as theories. When he was shocked in 1915 by the decline of Spencer's reputation, he doubtless felt that a final conclusion had been upset; his outlook was not philosophical but brooding and ruminative; and I believe that here, again, we get the image of Clym Yeobright, the young man ill-prepared to digest the learning of the great world, the provincial amateur who sees farther than his neighbors but who, if he had seen still farther, might not have accepted, *in an act of faith,* the Darwinian naturalism of his time. As late as 1922 he wrote in the "Apology" to *Late Lyrics and Earlier* that "when belief in witches of Endor is displacing the Darwinian theory and 'the truth that shall make you free,' men's minds appear, as above noted, to be moving backwards rather than on." The witches of Endor were doubtless presiding over the irrational passions of the War; but at any rate the going backwards instead of forwards indicates, I believe, a somewhat greater belief in one of the leading Victorian ideas, Progress, than is usually attributed to Hardy.

Perhaps Hardy's intense awareness of the folk-realism of his people modified the liberal optimism of his time, and checked his assent to the enthusiasm of his age at a particular stage, which he described as "evolutionary meliorism." Nevertheless, the reader of Hardy's novels gets a total impression in which this doctrine of "meliorism" is occasionally stated but in which it plays little part in terms of the characters and their plots. It has often been said that Hardy's two leading ideas, Necessity and Chance, Fate and "Crass Casualty," continue the Greek tradition; but it seems more likely that his Necessity is only Victorian Mechanism, and that Chance represents the occasional intercession into the mechanical routine of the universe, of Spencer's Unknowable.

It is a curious feature of Hardy's treatment of the Dorchester peasantry that not one of them is permitted to have a religious experience: their religious emotions are thoroughly "psychologized" and naturalistic. It would seem then that Hardy, like Clym, had reached an "advanced position" which forbade him to take seriously the religious life of his people. Their peculiar compound of pagan superstition and Christianity which issued in a simple miraculism (as opposed to Hardy's mechanism of fate interrupted by blind chance) he tended from the first to look at from the outside, where it seemed quaint and picturesque. This, of course, is not quite the whole story of Hardy's profound insight into human character, or of his mastery of dramatic form which he achieved in spite of technical limitations and of a high-falutin' prose style of which the best that can be said is that it has an occasional descriptive grandeur and a frequent bathos. (He once said that while poetry requires technique, prose writes itself—perhaps a British as well as a personal blindness.) I have offered this brief simplification of Hardy's intellectual "position" not as an explanation of his work, but merely as a pointer towards a certain kind of meaning that I have seen in his poetry.

II

One of Hardy's most powerful poems is "Nature's Questioning." It is written in a four-line stanza that seems characteristically to be derived from a hymn meter in the first two lines, but instead of completing the 4–3–4–3 stanza that the first two lines have led us to expect, he boldly finishes it off, 3–6, thus:

> *When I look forth at dawning, pool,*
> *   Field, flock, and lonely tree,*
> *   All seem to gaze at me*
> *Like chastened children sitting silent in school;*

> *Their faces dulled, constrained, and worn,*
> *   As though the master's ways*
> *   Through the long teaching days*
> *Had cowed them till their early zest was overborne.*

The Alexandrines in these stanzas are prosodically among the most successful in English: the sense overlaps the caesura, imparting to the structure a firmness that keeps the line from breaking down into two trimeters—the usual result of the attempt to write English hexameter. The poem proceeds, after two stanzas setting forth cosmic questions from nature:

> *Or come we of an Automaton*
> *   Unconscious of our pains? . . .*
> *   Or are we live remains*
> *Of Godhead dying downwards, brain and eye now gone?*

The two last lines are often cited as Hardy's most brilliant, and I think there can be no doubt of their magnificence. The phrase *now gone* could not be better: one is reminded of Henry James's tact concerning the presentation of supernatural beings in fiction, that "weak specifications" limit their credibility. *Now gone* is just specific enough, its colloquial tone bringing the idea of God within the range of familiarity without the risks of a too concrete image: brain and eye are not images, but rather objects denoted. The rhythm of the line seems to me to be masterly. The prevailing falling rhythm is suddenly shifted from "brain" to the end of the line, to a counter, mounting rhythm; moreover, the trimeter line latent in the hexameter becomes explicit—"Of Godhead dying downwards"—and the shock of *downwards* has the prolonged effect of the feminine ending; when the hexameter is resumed, *brain* strikes with tremendous force, with a secondary stress on *eye;* and *now gone* reads to my ear almost a spondee. In this last feature it seems to me that the final proof of the technical mastery appears (conscious in Hardy, or not). The rhythmic conflict in the line is never quite resolved. There has been a regular alternation of stressed and unstressed syllables, so that when we reach *now* we are under a strong compulsion to pass it over lightly; yet we cannot do it; the quantity of the syllable, reinforced by its rhetoric, stops us. Could we pass it lightly, *now gone* as an iambus would restore the prevailing pattern of mounting rhythm; as a spondee it suspends the conflict, the particular effect of meaning and rhythm being a kind of kinesthetic sensation that we soon discover that we have been attributing to the agony of the dying Godhead.

I do not apologize for laboring this point. Great passages of poetry are rare; because they are exceptionally rare in Hardy we must exert ourselves to the utmost to understand their value. There is nothing else in "Nature's Questioning" to reward our close attention—if we are looking for poetry; but there is a great deal that will illuminate our understanding of Hardy's poetry. The two last stanzas:

Or is it that some high Plan betides,
  As yet not understood,
  Of Evil stormed by Good,
We the Forlorn Hope over which Achievement strides?

Thus things around. No answerer I . . .
  Meanwhile the winds, and rains,
  And Earth's old glooms and pains
Are still the same, and Life and Death are neighbors nigh.

Now this poem as a whole fairly represents a use of metaphor practiced by certain Victorian poets. The inanimate "things around" that have asked the questions appear in the first stanza as pool, field, flock, and a tree whose sole quality is its loneliness; these objects quickly become school children, before they have been sufficiently particularized to be themselves. The transformation of the natural objects into persons is initiated with some degree

of tact in terms of simile—"Like chastened children"—
that we can accept because not too much is claimed for
it at that stage. But in the second stanza what appeared
to be simile becomes completed metaphor. We have here,
in the terms of Mr. I. A. Richards, an instance of metaphor
in which the "vehicle" replaces the "tenor": the natural
objects (tenor) are so weakly perceived that the children
(vehicle), who appear as the conveyance of their significance, cancel out the natural objects altogether; so that,
as the poem proceeds to the fourth stanza, we get a group
of inanimate objects as school children asking this question:

> *Has some vast Imbecility,*
> *Mighty to build and blend,*
> *But impotent to tend,*
> *Framed us in jest, and left us now to hazardry?*

Now Hardy is saying that the children are Nature, or
would like to say, since he is a nineteenth-century monist,
that they are also mechanically determined, as Nature is;
both human and nonhuman nature suffer the neglect of
the absentee God of Deism, who is:

> *Mighty to build and blend,*
> *But impotent to tend . . .*

This God is the schoolmaster of line two, stanza two;
here again the metaphorical vehicle replaces the tenor; and
in view of the deistic character of this God, the figure of
the "master," who is the personal, anthropomorphic rep-

resentation of the Unknowable, contradicts his logical significance: to render this God dramatically, Hardy has made him the God of theism, a personal, if not the Christian, God, but if he is the Automaton of stanza five, he is not equipped to teach a class; he cannot even be present if he is "impotent to tend."

Throughout this poem (and I should risk the guess, in most of the "philosophical" poems of Hardy) the margin of intelligible meaning achieved by the union of the tenor and the vehicle is very narrow. Even in the magnificent image of the "Godhead dying downwards" we get a certain degree of contradiction between tenor and vehicle: in order to say that God has left the universe to chance after setting it in motion, Hardy can merely present us with the theistic God as blind and imbecile.

So generally of Hardy it may perhaps be said that his "philosophy" tends to be a little beyond the range of his feeling: his abstractions are thus somewhat irresponsible, since he rarely shows us the experience that ought to justify them, that would give them substance, visibility, meaning. The visible embodiment of the meaning of "Nature's Questioning" ought doubtless to be "pool, field, flock, and lonely tree," which are not experienced objects of nature, but only universals of so thinly perceived quality that Hardy apparently had no trouble at all in absorbing them into the analogy of the school children; and likewise the schoolmaster is so thinly particularized that the next analogical development, master into God, is easy and unconvincing.

It is likely that other critics will from time to time examine other types of Hardy's verse; it will probably be many years before a comprehensive study of all his poetry can appear. I have a strong impression that the ballads, songs, and occasional lyrics, as well as the versified tales and the little ironic incidents of the *Satires of Circumstance,* exhibit the greatest freedom of sensibility of which Hardy, the poet, was capable: in the vast number of these slighter pieces Hardy is at his least philosophical; he is closer to the immediate subject, he is free to observe directly and to record the direct impression. But when he begins to think, when he begins to say what the impression, the observation, the incident means, he can only bring in his ill-digested philosophy—a *mélange* of Schopenhauer, Darwin, and Spencer, against a cosmological background of eighteenth-century Deism that he could not project imaginatively into his immediate experience.

Is this not the common situation of the Victorian poets and, with some differences, our predicament today? Our chief difference seems to consist in a greater awareness of the problem—not in its solution. Hardy's philosophical limitations permitted him to accept as "truth" Spencer's *Synthetic Philosophy,* with the result that he held to the mechanistic theories of his time with greater single-mindedness than Tennyson or Browning ever achieved. This single-mindedness probably kept him immune to the eclectic miscellany of easy solutions and speculations that his more sensitive contemporaries succumbed to. There can be no doubt that the poetic language of Hardy, particularly in poems like "God's Funeral" and "The Convergence of the Twain," achieves a weight and solidity that only Arnold of the Victorians—and then only in his best moments—could rival: perhaps his lack of a university training in literature permitted him to seize the language afresh, so that even his heavily Latinized vocabulary is capable of effects that a better educated poet in his age would have missed. It is as dangerous as it is meaningless to wish that a great poet might have either made up or suppressed his deficiencies. Had he been "better educated" he might have been like Browning or Swinburne—both men his inferiors; had he been worse educated, it is not inconceivable that he should have been even more like James Thomson (B.V.) than he was; but fortunately he was Thomas Hardy.

NARCISSUS AS NARCISSUS

I

O N THIS first occasion, which will probably be the last, of my writing about my own verse, I could plead in excuse the example of Edgar Allan Poe, who wrote about himself in an essay called "The Philosophy of Composition." But in our age the appeal to authority is weak, and I am of my age. What I happen to know about the poem that I shall discuss is limited. I remember merely my intention in writing it; I do not know whether the poem is good; and I do not know its obscure origins.

How does one happen to write a poem: where does it come from? That is the question asked by the psychologists or the geneticists of poetry. Of late I have not read any of the genetic theories very attentively: years ago I read one by Mr. Conrad Aiken; another, I think, by Mr. Robert Graves; but I have forgotten them. I am not ridiculing verbal mechanisms, dreams, or repressions as origins of poetry; all three of them and more besides may have a great deal to do with it. Nor should I ignore Mr. I. A. Richards, whose theories I have read a great deal: to him a poem seems to induce a kind of ideal harmony out of the greatest number of our appetites, which ordinarily jangle, and the reader gets the same harmony or "ordering of the mind" second-hand—only it is really as good as first-hand since the poet differs from the mere reader by the fine hair of his talent for constructing appetitive harmonies in words. While this theory may be false, I can only say that, given a few premises which I shall not discuss, it is logical: I do not care whether it is false or true. Other psychological theories say a good deal about compensation. A poem is an indirect effort of a shaky man to justify himself to happier men, or to present a superior account of his relation to a world that allows him but little certainty, and would allow equally little to the happier men if they did not wear blinders—according to the poet. For example, a poet might be a man who could not get enough self-justification out of being an automobile salesman (whose certainty is a fixed quota of cars every month) to rest comfortably upon it. So the poet, who wants to be something that he cannot be, and is a failure in plain life, makes up fictitious versions of his predicament that are interesting even to other persons because nobody is a perfect automobile salesman. Everybody, alas, suffers a little . . . I constantly read this kind of criticism of my own verse. According to its doctors, my one intransigent desire is to have been a Confederate general, and because I could not or would not become anything else, I set up for poet and began to invent fictions about the personal ambitions that my society has no use for.

Although a theory may not be "true," it may make certain insights available for a while; and I have deemed it proper to notice theories of the genetic variety because a poet talking about himself is often expected, as the best authority, to explain the origins of his poems. But persons interested in origins are seldom quick to use them. Poets, in their way, are practical men; they are interested in results. What is the poem, after it is written? That is the question. Not where it came from, or why. The Why and Where can never get beyond the guessing stage because, in the language of those who think it can, poetry cannot be brought to "laboratory conditions." The only real evidence that any critic may bring before his gaze is the finished poem. For some reason most critics have a hard time fixing their minds directly under their noses, and before they see the object that is there they use a telescope upon the horizon to see where it came from. They are woodcutters who do their job by finding out where the ore came from in the iron of the steel of the blade of the axe that Jack built. I do not say that this procedure is without its own contributory insights; but the insights are merely contributory and should not replace the poem, which is the object upon which they must be focused. A poem may be an instance of morality, of social conditions, of psychological history; it may instance all its qualities, but never one of them alone, nor any two or three; nor ever less than all.

Genetic theories, I gather, have been cherished academically with detachment. Among "critics" they have been useless and not quite disinterested: I have myself found them applicable to the work of poets whom I do not like. That is the easiest way.

I say all this because it seems to me that my verse or anybody else's is merely a way of knowing something: if the poem is a real creation, it is a kind of knowledge that we did not possess before. It is not knowledge "about" something else; the poem is the fullness of that knowledge. We know the particular poem, not what it says that we can restate. In a manner of speaking, the poem is its own knower, neither poet nor reader knowing anything that the poem says apart from the words of the poem. I have expressed this view elsewhere in other terms, and it has been accused of aestheticism or art for art's sake. But let the reader recall the historic position of Catholicism: *nulla salus extra ecclesiam.* That must be religion*ism.* There is probably nothing wrong with art for art's sake if we take the phrase seriously, and not take it to mean the kind of poetry written in England forty years ago. Religion always ought to transcend any of its particular uses; and likewise the true art for art's sake view can be held only by persons who are always looking for things that they can respect apart from use (though they may be useful), like poems, fly-rods, and formal gardens. . . . These are negative postulates, and I am going to illustrate them with some commentary on a poem called "Ode to the Confederate Dead."

II

That poem is "about" solipsism, a philosophical doctrine which says that we create the world in the act of perceiving it; or about Narcissism, or any other *ism* that denotes the failure of the human personality to function objectively in nature and society. Society (and "nature" as modern society constructs it) appears to offer limited fields for the exercise of the whole man, who wastes his energy piecemeal over separate functions that ought to come under a unity of being. (Until the last generation, only certain women were whores, having been set aside as special instances of sex amid a social scheme that held the general belief that sex must be part of a whole; now the general belief is that sex must be special.) Without unity we get the remarkable self-consciousness of our age. Everybody is talking about this evil, and a great many persons know what ought to be done to correct it. As a citizen I have my own prescription, but as a poet I am concerned with the experience of "solipsism." And an experience *of* it is not quite the same thing as a philosophical statement *about* it.

I should have trouble connecting solipsism and the Confederate dead in a rational thesis; I should make a fool of myself in the discussion, because I know no more of the Confederate dead or of solipsism than hundreds of other people. (Possibly less: the dead Confederates may be presumed to have a certain privacy; and as for solipsism, I blush in the presence of philosophers, who know all about Bishop Berkeley; I use the term here in its strict etymology.) And if I call this interest in one's ego Narcissism, I make myself a logical ignoramus, and I take liberties with mythology. I use Narcissism to mean only preoccupation with self; it may be love or hate. But a good psychiatrist knows that it means self-love only, and otherwise he can talk about it more coherently, knows more about it than I shall ever hope or desire to know. He would look at me professionally if I uttered the remark that the modern squirrel cage of our sensibility, the extreme introspection of our time, has anything whatever to do with the Confederate dead.

But when the doctor looks at literature it is a question whether he sees it: the sea boils and pigs have wings because in poetry all things are possible—if you are man enough. They are possible because in poetry the disparate elements are not combined in logic, which can join things only under certain categories and under the law of contradiction; they are combined in poetry rather as experience, and experience has decided to ignore logic, except perhaps as another field of experience. Experience means conflict, our natures being what they are, and conflict means drama. Dramatic experience is not logical; it may be subdued to the kind of coherence that we indicate when we speak, in criticism, of form. Indeed, as experience, this conflict is always a logical contradiction, or philosophically an antinomy. Serious poetry deals with the fundamental conflicts that cannot be logically resolved: we can state the conflicts rationally, but reason does not relieve us of them. Their only final coherence is the formal re-creation of art, which "freezes" the experience as permanently as a logical formula, but without, like the formula, leaving all but the logic out.

Narcissism and the Confederate dead cannot be connected logically, or even historically; even were the connection an historical fact, they would not stand connected as art, for no one experiences raw history. The proof of the connection must lie, if anywhere, in the experienced conflict which is the poem itself. Since one set of references for the conflict is the historic Confederates, the poem, if it is successful, is a certain section of history made into experience, but only on this occasion, and on these terms: even the author of the poem has no experience of its history apart from the occasion and the terms.

It will be understood that I do not claim even a partial success in the junction of the two "ideas" in the poem that I am about to discuss. I am describing an intention, and the labor of revising the poem—a labor spread over ten years—fairly exposes the lack of confidence that I have felt and still feel in it. All the tests of its success in style and versification would come in the end to a single test, an answer, yes or no, to the question: Assuming that the Confederates and Narcissus are not yoked together by mere violence, has the poet convinced the reader that, on the specific occasion of this poem, there is a necessary yet hitherto undetected relation between them? By necessary I mean dramatically relevant, a relation "discovered" in terms of the particular occasion, not historically argued or philosophically deduced. Should the question that I have

just asked be answered yes, then this poem or any other
with its specific problem could be said to have form: what
was previously a merely felt quality of life has been raised
to the level of experience—it has become specific, local,
dramatic, "formal"—that is to say, *in*-formed.

III

The structure of the Ode is simple. Figure to yourself
a man stopping at the gate of a Confederate graveyard on
a late autumn afternoon. The leaves are falling; his first
impressions bring him the "rumor of mortality"; and the
desolation barely allows him, at the beginning of the
second stanza, the conventionally heroic surmise that the
dead will enrich the earth, "where these memories grow."
From those quoted words to the end of that passage he
pauses for a baroque meditation on the ravages of time,
concluding with the figure of the "blind crab." This crea-
ture has mobility but no direction, energy but no purpose-
ful world to use it in: in the entire poem there are only
two explicit symbols for the looked-in ego; the crab is the
first and less explicit symbol, a mere hint, a planting of
the idea that will become overt in its second instance—the
jaguar towards the end. The crab is the first intimation of
the nature of the moral conflict upon which the drama of
the poem develops: the cut-off-ness of the modern "intellectual man" from the world.

The next long passage or "strophe," beginning "You
know who have waited by the wall," states the other term

of the conflict. It is the theme of heroism, not merely moral heroism, but heroism in the grand style, elevating even death from mere physical dissolution into a formal ritual: this heroism is a formal ebullience of the human spirit in an entire society, not private, romantic illusion— something better than moral heroism, great as that may be, for moral heroism, being personal and individual, may be achieved by certain men in all ages, even ages of decadence. But the late Hart Crane's commentary, in a letter, is better than any I can make; he described the theme as the "theme of chivalry, a tradition of excess (not literally excess, rather active faith) which cannot be perpetuated in the fragmentary cosmos of today—'those desires which should be yours tomorrow,' but which, you know, will not persist nor find any way into action."

The structure then is the objective frame for the tension between the two themes, "active faith" which has decayed, and the "fragmentary cosmos" which surrounds us. (I must repeat here that this is not a philosophical thesis; it is an analytical statement of a conflict that is concrete within the poem.) In contemplating the heroic theme the man at the gate never quite commits himself to the illusion of its availability to him. The most that he can allow himself is the fancy that the blowing leaves are charging soldiers, but he rigorously returns to the refrain: "Only the wind"—or the "leaves flying." I suppose it is a commentary on our age that the man at the gate never quite achieves the illusion that the leaves are heroic men, so that he may identify himself with them, as Keats and Shelley too easily

and too beautifully did with nightingales and west winds.
More than this, he cautions himself, reminds himself re-
peatedly of his subjective prison, his solipsism, by breaking
off the half-illusion and coming back to the refrain of
wind and leaves—a refrain that, as Hart Crane said, is
necessary to the "subjective continuity."

These two themes struggle for mastery up to the passage,

> *We shall say only the leaves whispering*
> *In the improbable mist of nightfall—*

which is near the end. It will be observed that the passage
begins with a phrase taken from the wind-leaves refrain—
the signal that it has won. The refrain has been fused with
the main stream of the man's reflections, dominating them;
and he cannot return even to an ironic vision of the
heroes. There is nothing but death, the mere naturalism
of death at that—spiritual extinction in the decay of the
body. Autumn and the leaves are death; the men who ex-
emplified in a grand style an "active faith" are dead; there
are only the leaves.

Shall we then worship death . . .

> . . . *set up the grave*
> *In the house? The ravenous grave . . .*

that will take us before our time? The question is not answered, although as a kind of morbid romanticism it
might, if answered affirmatively, provide the man with an
illusory escape from his solipsism; but he cannot accept it.

Nor has he been able to live in his immediate world, the fragmentary cosmos. There is no practical solution, no solution offered for the edification of moralists. (To those who may identify the man at the gate with the author of the poem I would say: He differs from the author in not accepting a "practical solution," for the author's dilemma is perhaps not quite so exclusive as that of the meditating man.) The main intention of the poem has been to make dramatically visible the conflict, to concentrate it, to present it, in Mr. R. P. Blackmur's phrase, as "experienced form"—not as a logical dilemma.

The closing image, that of the serpent, is the ancient symbol of time, and I tried to give it the credibility of the commonplace by placing it in a mulberry bush—with the faint hope that the silkworm would somehow be implicit. But time is also death. If that is so, then space, or the Becoming, is life; and I believe there is not a single spatial symbol in the poem. "Sea-space" is allowed the "blind crab"; but the sea, as appears plainly in the passage beginning, "Now that the salt of their blood . . ." is life only in so far as it is the source of the lowest forms of life, the source perhaps of all life, but life undifferentiated, half-way between life and death. This passage is a contrasting inversion of the conventional

> . . . *inexhaustible bodies that are not*
> *Dead, but feed the grass . . .*

the reduction of the earlier, literary conceit to a more naturalistic figure derived from modern biological speculation. These "buried Caesars" will not bloom in the hyacinth but will only make saltier the sea.

The wind-leaves refrain was added to the poem in 1930, nearly five years after the first draft was written. I felt that the danger of adding it was small because, implicit in the long strophes of meditation, the ironic commentary on the vanished heroes was already there, giving the poem such dramatic tension as it had in the earlier version. The refrain makes the commentary more explicit, more visibly dramatic, and renders quite plain, as Hart Crane intimated, the subjective character of the imagery throughout. But there was another reason for it, besides the increased visualization that it imparts to the dramatic conflict. It "times" the poem better, offers the reader frequent pauses in the development of the two themes, allows him occasions of assimilation; and on the whole—this was my hope and intention—the refrain makes the poem seem longer than it is and thus eases the concentration of imagery— without, I hope, sacrificing a possible effect of concentration.

IV

I have been asked why I called the poem an ode. I first called it an elegy. It is an ode only in the sense in which Cowley in the seventeenth century misunderstood the real structure of the Pindaric ode. Not only are the meter and rhyme without fixed pattern, but in another feature the poem is even further removed from Pindar than Abraham Cowley was: a purely subjective meditation would not even in Cowley's age have been called an ode. I suppose in so calling it I intended an irony: the scene of the poem is not a public celebration, it is a lone man by a gate.

The dominant rhythm is "mounting," the dominant meter iambic pentameter varied with six-, four-, and three-stressed lines; but this was not planned in advance for variety. I adapted the meter to the effect desired at the moment. The model for the irregular rhyming was "Lycidas," but other models could have served. The rhymes in a given strophe I tried to adjust to the rhythm and the texture of feeling and image. For example, take this passage in the second strophe:

> *Autumn is desolation in the plot*
> *Of a thousand acres where these memories grow*
> *From the inexhaustible bodies that are not*
> *Dead, but feed the grass row after rich row.*
> *Think of the autumns that have come and gone!—*
> *Ambitious November with the humors of the year,*
> *With a particular zeal for every slab,*
> *Staining the uncomfortable angels that rot*
> *On the slabs, a wing chipped here, an arm there:*
> *The brute curiosity of an angel's stare*
> *Turns you, like them, to stone,*
> *Transforms the heaving air*
> *Till plunged to a heavier world below*
> *You shift your sea-space blindly*
> *Heaving, turning like the blind crab.*

There is rhymed with *year* (to many persons, perhaps, only a half-rhyme), and I hoped the reader would unconsciously assume that he need not expect further use of that sound for some time. So when the line, "The brute curiosity of an angel's stare," comes a moment later, rhyming with *year-there,* I hoped that the violence of image would be further reinforced by the repetition of a sound that was no longer expected. I wanted the shock to be heavy; so I felt that I could not afford to hurry the reader away from it until he had received it in full. The next two lines carry on the image at a lower intensity: the rhyme, "Transforms the heaving *air,*" prolongs the moment of attention upon that passage, while at the same time it ought to begin dissipating the shock, both by the introduction of a new image and by reduction of the "meaning" to a pattern of sound, the ere-rhymes. I calculated that the third use of that sound (stare) would be a surprise, the fourth (air) a monotony. I purposely made the end words of the third from last and last lines—*below* and *crab*—delayed rhymes for *row* and *slab,* the last being an internal and half-dissonant rhyme for the sake of bewilderment and incompleteness, qualities by which the man at the gate is at the moment possessed.

This is elementary but I cannot vouch for its success. As the dramatic situation of the poem is the tension that I have already described, so the rhythm is an attempt at a series of "modulations" back and forth between a formal regularity, for the heroic emotion, and a broken rhythm, with scattering imagery, for the failure of that emotion.

This is "imitative form," which Yvor Winters deems a vice worth castigation. I have pointed out that the passage, "You know who have waited by the wall," presents the heroic theme of "active faith"; it will be observed that the rhythm, increasingly after "You who have waited for the angry resolution," is almost perfectly regular iambic, with only a few initial inversions and weak endings. The passage is meant to convey a plenary vision, the actual presence, of the exemplars of active faith: the man at the gate at that moment is nearer to realizing them than at any other in the poem; hence the formal rhythm. But the vision breaks down; the wind-leaves refrain supervenes; and the next passage, "Turn your eyes to the immoderate past," is the irony of the preceding realization. With the self-conscious historical sense he turns his eyes into the past. The next passage after this, beginning, "You hear the shout..." is the failure of the vision in both phases, the pure realization and the merely historical. He cannot "see" the heroic virtues; there is wind, rain, leaves. But there is sound; for a moment he deceives himself with it. It is the noise of the battles that he has evoked. Then comes the figure of the rising sun of those battles; he is "lost in that orient of the thick and fast," and he curses his own moment, "the setting sun." The "setting sun" I tried to use as a triple image, for the decline of the heroic age and for the actual scene of late afternoon, the latter being not only natural desolation but spiritual desolation as well. Again for a moment he thinks he hears the battle shout, but only for a moment; then the silence reaches him.

Corresponding to the disintegration of the vision just described, there has been a breaking down of the formal rhythm. The complete breakdown comes with the images of the "mummy" and the "hound bitch." (*Hound* bitch because the hound is a hunter, participant of a formal ritual.) The failure of the vision throws the man back upon himself, but upon himself he cannot bring to bear the force of sustained imagination. He sees himself in random images (random to him, deliberate with the author) of something lower than he ought to be: the human image is only that of preserved death; but if he is alive he is an old hunter, dying. The passages about the mummy and the bitch are deliberately brief—slight rhythmic stretches. (These are the only verses I have written for which I thought of the movement first, then cast about for the symbols.)

I believe the term modulation denotes in music the uninterrupted shift from one key to another: I do not know the term for change of rhythm without change of measure. I wish to describe a similar change in verse rhythm; it may be convenient to think of it as modulation of a certain kind. At the end of the passage that I have been discussing the final words are "Hears the wind only." The phrase closes the first main division of the poem. I have loosely called the longer passages strophes, and if I were hardy enough to impose the classical organization of the lyric ode upon a baroque poem, I should say that these words bring to an end the Strophe, after which must come the next main division, or Antistrophe, which was often employed to answer the matter set forth in the Strophe or to present it from another point of view. And that is precisely the significance of the next main division, beginning: "Now that the salt of their blood . . ." But I wanted this second division of the poem to arise out of the collapse of the first. It is plain that it would not have suited my purpose to round off the first section with some sort of formal rhythm; so I ended it with an unfinished line. The next division must therefore begin by finishing that line, not merely in meter but with an integral rhythm. I will quote the passage:

> *The hound bitch*
> *Toothless and dying, in a musty cellar*
> Hears the wind only.
>
> Now that the salt of their blood
> *Stiffens the saltier oblivion of the sea,*
> *Seals the malignant purity of the flood. . . .*

The caesura, after *only,* is thus at the middle of the third foot. (I do not give a full stress to *wind,* but attribute a "hovering stress" to *wind* and the first syllable of *only.*) The reader expects the foot to be completed by the stress on the next word, *Now,* as in a sense it is; but the phrase, "Now that the salt of their blood," is also the beginning of a new movement; it is two "dactyls" continuing more broadly the falling rhythm that has prevailed. But with the finishing off of the line with *blood,* the mounting rhythm is restored; the whole line from *Hears* to *blood* is actually an iambic pentameter with liberal inversions and substitutions that were expected to create a counter-rhythm within the line. From the caesura on, the rhythm is new; but it has—or was expected to have—an organic relation to the preceding rhythm; and it signals the rise of a new statement of the theme.

I have gone into this passage in detail—I might have chosen another—not because I think it is successful, but because I labored with it; if it is a failure, or even an uninteresting success, it ought to offer as much technical instruction to other persons as it would were it both successful and interesting. But a word more: the broader movement introduced by the new rhythm was meant to correspond, as a sort of Antistrophe, to the earlier formal movement beginning, "You know who have waited by the wall." It is a new formal movement with new feeling and new imagery. The heroic but precarious illusion of the earlier movement has broken down into the personal symbols of the mummy and the hound; the pathetic fallacy of the leaves as charging soldiers and the conventional "buried Caesar" theme have become rotten leaves and dead bodies wasting in the earth, to return after long erosion to the sea. In the midst of this naturalism, what shall the man say? What shall all humanity say in the presence of decay? The two themes, then, have been struggling for mastery; the structure of the poem thus exhibits the development of two formal passages that contrast the two themes. The two formal passages break down, the first shading into the second ("Now that the salt of their blood..."), the second one concluding with the figure of

the jaguar, which is presented in a distracted rhythm left
suspended at the end from a weak ending—the word
victim. This figure of the jaguar is the only explicit rendering of the Narcissus motif in the poem, but instead of a
youth gazing into a pool, a predatory beast stares at a
jungle stream, and leaps to devour himself.

The next passage begins:

> *What shall we say who have knowledge*
> *Carried to the heart?*

This is Pascal's war between heart and head, between
finesse and *géométrie*. Should the reader care to think of
these lines as the gathering up of the two themes, now
fused, into a final statement, I should see no objection to
calling it the Epode. But upon the meaning of the lines
from here to the end there is no need for further commentary. I have talked about the structure of the poem,
not its quality. One can no more find the quality of one's
own verse than one can find its value, and to try to find
either is like looking into a glass for the effect that one's
face has upon other persons.

If anybody ever wished to know anything about this
poem that he could not interpret for himself, I suspect
that he is still in the dark. I cannot believe that I have
illuminated the difficulties that some readers have found
in the style. But then I cannot, have never been able to,
see any difficulties of that order. The poem has been much
revised. I still think there is much to be said for the orig-
inal *barter* instead of *yield* in the second line, and for

Novembers instead of *November* in line fifteen. The revisions were not undertaken for the convenience of the reader but for the poem's own clarity, so that, word, phrase, line, passage, the poem might at worst come near its best expression.

PROCRUSTES AND THE POETS

CRITICISM OF the novel still faces the insuperable difficulties described by Percy Lubbock in *The Craft of
Fiction* twenty years ago, yet the problem of the novel
lacks a special difficulty that the critic of poetry may never
lose sight of. That difficulty is the intricate use of language
as symbolism. Although I do not mean to say that the
critic of the novel needs no unusual powers, he chiefly
needs first of all good sense; for novels—even novels by
Mrs. Woolf—are action; and action may succeed well
enough without trying for any of the ultimate effects of
language. Language for action and language for symbolism
are not, of course, generically different, but they tend towards great divergence. The symbolic use of language demands of the critic not only unusual intelligence but very
special powers of reading. Mr. Daiches seems to me to
be primarily a critic of general ideas, and his new book [1]
is less successful than his recent *The Novel and the
Modern World*.

Mr. Daiches is better at backgrounds, influences, forces
than he is at the poetic text. That general interest, I believe, has made him a better reader of novels than of

[1] *Poetry and the Modern World: A Study of Poetry in England between 1900 and 1939*, by David Daiches. (Chicago, 1940).

poems. His general test of the value of modern poets is social "relevance" and social "truths"—not Truth, as he explicitly warns us. It ought to be said at once that, although he is in some general sense a Marxist, he offers us none of the fanatical crudities of the extreme Marxists of the last decade. There is even evidence in this book that he enjoys the advantages of a classical education; he has a detachment which some of the English Marxists achieved in their understanding of political ideas and which gave to their literary criticism a maturity of judgment not conspicuous in most of their American contemporaries: a refusal to take up intellectually suicidal "positions," from which, since they could not move, they could not grow.

There are many literary judgments in this book which expose the limitations of any sort of doctrine of social or historical relevance, however intelligently it may be used. I will cite only three of them. "It is Yeats's structural ability," says Mr. Daiches, "and his superb gift of phrase which enable him to transform private mutterings into great poetry." But according to Mr. Daiches's general theory, private mutterings cannot be great poetry; the mutterings must have social relevance. If they are great poetry, are they still private mutterings even though they may lack Mr. Daiches's kind of relevance? Mr. Daiches is perplexed by what he calls Yeats's "fantastic philosophy," which he cannot accept, because it is not "relevant." There has always been in the Marxist, and even in the more general sociological, criticism of literature, a concealed neo-classicism: the doctrine that the poet begins with sound and

acceptable ideas and dresses them up with a "superb gift
of phrase." But Mr. Daiches is properly overwhelmed by
Yeats's genius and power; he cannot dismiss him; yet he is
puzzled because the poetry cannot be distinguished from
ideas that he finds nonsensical, even "crazy." Again, Mr.
Daiches is strongly inclined to dismiss from the Eliot canon
everything since "The Hollow Men"—everything, that is
to say, since the religious phase which begins with "Ash
Wednesday." Since that phase began, Eliot has lost everything except his powers of "organization." Mr. Daiches
simply does not like, does not see as "relevant," what Eliot
has been using those powers to organize. There is here
something like a wilful stultification of perception on the
part of a critic who can, outside the circle of his prejudices,
be both sensitive and astute. Yet, on the whole, Mr.
Daiches's general intelligence serves him well until he
comes to C. Day Lewis, towards the end of the book: the
chapter on Day Lewis can be described only as a critical
collapse. He takes seriously a third-rate poet, because the
verse points to "ideas" that Mr. Daiches likes.

There is Yeats with his "fantastic philosophy" and his
great poetry. There is Day Lewis with his—to Mr. Daiches
—sound philosophy and his—to me—bad poetry. This is
our common predicament as readers of poetry, and it indicates, I believe, the direction one must take to find the
chief problem of poetic criticism. If Mr. Daiches cannot
deal with it in terms of his method, should he not try to
get a new one?

I think it is possible to discern the point at which Mr.

Daiches slides off this problem. We watch him while, like a detective hero, he absently picks up the clue, then lays it down and moves on. The clue is the problem of "multiple belief." His discussion of this problem and his frequent references to it represent the nearest approach to subtlety in Mr. Daiches's reading of the modern poets. (I should like to see acknowledgments to Cleanth Brooks, Empson, Ransom, and Blackmur, who do this sort of reading still better.) Mr. Daiches's contribution to our understanding of multiple belief, or of "ambivalent attitudes," consists in a simplified framework of historical reference. "There are thus," he says, "three groups—those who met the problem by limitation of the existing tradition, those who met it by going back to an older, long abandoned tradition, and those who tried to create a new tradition." It is an illuminating scheme: in the first group, the Imagists; in the second, Eliot; in the third, Auden and, surprisingly, Yeats—because he must go in somewhere. Yet in every sense but that of "style," in the later poems, Yeats went back to an older tradition. Perhaps Mr. Daiches fails to identify it because he cannot find it in an historical period and a social background.

The joker is the word tradition. What is it? Mr. Daiches seems to assume that in the first group it is merely literary; in the second, literary and religious; in the third, literary, political, and social. In the qualities of the third group, we see the outlines of the new and complete tradition. (Without religion it is nevertheless complete.) To what extent do the modern poets fit into this framework? To a very slight extent, if we ascribe to it a real objective validity, if we make it more than the tool of a provisional insight. Yeats's obstinate refusal to fit in ought to warn us that the critical value of Mr. Daiches's three groups is seriously impaired if we look upon them as exclusive possibilities of poetic sensibility. And by that phrase I mean a restraining determinant outside us, something ascertainable in the historical process apart from the poetry.

Mr. Daiches is aware of the danger without being quite free from it. It seems to me quite plain that he pushes an illuminating insight beyond its true use, to the point where it becomes a dogmatic injunction on the poets to heed the demands of "relevance." There is the tendency to force the complex poetic language into simple correspondence with social and historical ideas that Mr. Daiches would like to fix in advance: he seems to know better than the poets what they should have done about his three attitudes towards "tradition."

It is this external view, I believe, that keeps him from making as much of the problem of "multiple belief" as he might otherwise have done; and to have made more of that problem might have led him to a quite different conclusion—that his framework ought to fit the poets, not the poets the framework, that the history must prove itself in the poetry, not the poetry in the history. He misses the multiple effects of a difficult historical situation in the poets themselves. In calling this "situation" historical, we are confessing that its reality is inchoate rather than formed: all that we know about it, all that we have the

evidence to demonstrate, we know through the poetry itself. For it is there that it enjoys the only coherent reality
that we can experience. By trying to fit the poets into his
groups, he sets up as the test of their value, not some
standard taken from the poetry, but the degree of their
conformity to an external reference which exists on the
personal authority of Mr. Daiches's assertion. He remarks
that Eliot in "The Waste Land" tried "to solve the cultural problem of his time." Would it not be more within
the range of what we actually know to assume that Eliot
was trying to write as good a poem as he could, with materials that interested him? What were these materials?
Was the cultural problem of our time already in them? I
doubt it. If there is a cultural problem in what "The
Waste Land" actually says, did not the poem rather create
the problem than solve it?

In what sense does poetry solve problems? Possibly none
but its own. Beyond that, it is a question that I cannot
undertake to answer here; yet I think we may justly feel
that Mr. Daiches is asking for an answer that neither he
nor anyone else is going to get. He is asking the modern
poets to assent to his hope of a special solution to the social and political problem—which is likely to be another
sort of problem altogether, more difficult than sociology
and politics. (He seems to feel that the chief problem of
our time, whatever it is, raises the moral question only
when certain poets, perhaps Eliot and Yeats, refuse to see
it socially and politically; that is, such poets tend to be
irresponsible, their ideas tend to "irrelevance.") What Mr.

Daiches's own solution is cannot detain us, for it is not explicitly stated in this book; it exists as an assumed body of ideas to which reference can be conveniently made. Beyond the general insight that poetry "refers" to life, his criterion of relevance is a variety of the "pseudo-reference" that Yvor Winters has found in the experimental poets: it is reference to a standard which has not been objectively located.

When Mr. Daiches asks whether a poet or a poem is "relevant," may we not return the question: relevant to what? The strict answer must be: relevant to his analysis of the "historical situation," relevant to what he would like to see the poets do—not necessarily to what they have done. His general point of view, then, is some kind of social and political determinism, or perhaps a "cultural" determinism, of the arts; the broader term indicates Mr. Daiches's genuine awareness of the complexities of the critical problem.

Although he is a good reader of poetry, quite good enough to be frankly baffled by the failure of the poets to make up their minds, he is exasperated at the conflict and the multiplicity of belief and attitude that the poets appear to be unwilling or unable to simplify. Multiple belief points for Mr. Daiches to the external complexities of the social *milieu*—complexities outside the poetry. So the background, the situation in which the poet finds himself, is the objective material for study. The poetry is the subjective pointer towards the external situation. *Poetry and the Modern World* is an excellent historical essay from a

school of critics who have dominated poetic criticism since
the First World War. But there is a question that I believe
this school should begin to ask: Does not the doctrine of
relevance tend to return the formed experience of poetry
and the other arts to the flux of history? To which, then,
to the poetry or to the critic's historical picture, are we to
give the greater authority? Mr. Daiches as critic uses with
great competence a method that betrays him, as it betrays
its other adherents, into the assumption of an omniscience
to which he would not lay claim as a man.

NINE POETS: 1937[1]

JUST TEN years ago Laura Riding and Robert Graves, in
A Survey of Modernist Poetry, a book that has been
grossly neglected, made this illuminating statement:

The whole trend of modern poetry is toward treating poetry
like a very sensitive substance which succeeds better when
allowed to crystallize by itself than when put into prepared
moulds: this is why modern criticism, deprived of its discus-
sions of questions of form, tries to replace them by obscure
metaphysical reflections.

This judgment applies to criticism as a whole today, with
the honorable exceptions of Mr. Winters, Mr. Ransom,
and Mr. Blackmur. For the Marxists and the Humanists,
who have dominated recent criticism, have only seemed
to make the metaphysical reflections less obscure by making them crude, and they have got rid of the sensitive substance only by trying to read into poetry dogmatic subject
matters. The technical analysis of verse is no forwarder

[1] *Salt Water Ballads*, by Robert P. Tristram Coffin. *Address to the Liv-
ing*, by John Holmes. *They Say the Forties*, by Howard Mumford Jones.
The Emperor Heart, by Laurence Whistler. *Darkling Plain*, by Sara Bard
Field. *Poems*, by C. F. MacIntyre. *Monticello and Other Poems*, by
Lawrence Lee. *The Sleeping Fury*, by Louise Bogan. *From Jordan's De-
light*, by R. P. Blackmur.

today—with the honorable exceptions that have not yet affected the popular reviewers—than it was in the age of free-verse.

The poetry of our time must inevitably suffer from this lack, though it would be rash to assume that a more rigorous criticism, ten years ago, would have made it harder for our inferior poets to write: it would have made it considerably harder for them to write today as Messrs. Coffin, Holmes, and Jones do, in facile reproductions of certain "period styles" of the middle 'twenties. Mr. Coffin, with some degree of tenacious humility, has made of Mr. Frost's a period style; Mr. Holmes has taken Stephen Vincent Benet's "style," made it hortatory and wholesome, spiritually problemed and "American"; and Mr. Jones—alas, what can be said of Mr. Howard Mumford Jones? Let Mr. Jones speak for himself:

O great white Christ, beautiful and compassionate,
Thou who takest away the sins of the world,
Thou clean bright sword, thou pillar, thou banner un-
    furled
At morning, imperial and importunate,
Thou symbol beyond all creeds, all forms of state,
Thou from whose face corruption and lust are swirled
Into nothingness, whose strong fingers are curled
About the earth, upholding it—though we come late
Into an evil time, and though decay
Has been our father, and despair our mother,

Though our hearts are set hard against thee, and our lips
Deny thee, and we have scourged thee again with whips
Who art our victim and our torture and our brother,
We cry unto thee from the blood and tears of this day.

It is not so much period style as period sentiment. The time is rather too easily evil, decay and despair an ancestry a little too fashionable, and altogether Christ is too various and stagy and the blood and tears a little too much the rabbits out of the hat, to convince us that Mr. Jones is not really spoofing us. I trust that it is not necessary to go far into this matter. Whose blood and tears? Where did they come from? Mr. Jones prefers the sonnet, but he occasionally gives us a lyric, and here is the last stanza of "You That Were Beautiful":

> *You that were wonderful,*
> *Where have you gone,*
> *Whose breast of ivory*
> *Like silver shone?*

This is the style of the poets in Godey's *Lady's Book*. It alternates with the styles of Eliot and of Cummings. Cummings:

> *...the din*
> *of female voices lifts and explodes above*
> *the sudden sandwiches...*

Eliot:

> *When the arteries harden, a picture, a phrase, a face?*
> *Shall I tell them the bitter truth? Would it be worth-*
> *while?*

Would it be worthwhile to remind Mr. Jones that for years he has held up Eliot as an excellent example of fraud? I am at a loss to understand why the only amusing verse in this book—a kind of harsh *vers de société,* as if the late Calvin Coolidge had stooped to the *genre*—comes right out of Eliot, while the notes in other strains sound like the magazine verse of eighty years ago, a period style not quite in tone with the Eliot-Cummings era. Couldn't Mr. Jones have used, for his *vers de société,* a model a little nearer in time to Godey's? There was William Mackworth Praed, good enough for anybody.

If I have been hard on Mr. Jones, I can only plead in defense the mild discouragement of a reader who has looked for a reason why this verse should have been printed, and looked in vain. Mr. Jones will amuse us for a few lines, then get serious—or worse, bathetic. In sonnet V of *The Forties* a sequence about what is sometimes called modern disillusionment, in which Eliot, Hemingway, and Faulkner are blamed for a good deal of Mr. Jones's woe, there is a kind of scramble of allusions which appear only to remind us that Mr. Jones has read Shakespeare, Donne, and Keats: as if—to use a Homeric simile—the late Henry Clay Frick were quoting the Beatitudes at a directors' meeting. The quality of Mr. Jones's—what

shall I say—sensibility?—I forbear to phrase, and leave it
to the reader by quoting sonnet V entire:

> *Go feed your brain on bitterness, feed it full,*
> *Give wormwood to your heart, and fold on fold,*
> *Bid the snake, custom, curl its treacherous gold*
> *About the secret places of your skull.*
> *It is therefore we are leaders, we who are dull*
> *But eminent. Our shining names are told,*
> *Our notable acts, our virtues are enrolled*
> *In* Who's Who in America *for you to cull.*
>
> *But do not meet meanwhile with your own ghost*
> *Who died before the god, Success, was born,*
> *For he will greet you with such wild surmise*
> *Flushing his cheeks and startling in his eyes*
> *As will revive the ambition, the pain, the lost*
> *Sweet passion and the beautiful young scorn.*

Mr. Laurence Whistler, in his third volume, *The Emperor Heart,* comes highly recommended by the present
poet-laureate, Mr. John Masefield, for whom these verses
are "unlike the writing of any other" and for whom Mr.
Whistler's "thought is occupied with beauty." That is a
pleasant subject to be occupied with. But I have a distinct
impression, gleaned from more than casual study of his
book, that Mr. Whistler's beauty is a little more local, in
time and place, than Mr. Masefield's phrase would seem
to allow it to be. The beauty seems to me to be pre-War

English Georgian and to exist in the innocent notations of
the pretty park which is rural England, the corn, the wind,
the spring, and the sheep, to say nothing of the distant
manor house, nicely indicated but not quite realized in a
rhythm or imagery that we have not seen before. But the
evil times have marked Mr. Whistler: there is here and
there a taint of the wicked metaphysical style:

> *O put my arms about the vernal waist*
> *And close my eyes upon the immortal womb.*
> *Rest, rest, distracted frame, against the core*
> *Of all this darkening love that is your home—*

But I should not want anybody to think that Mr. Whistler
is always so uncomfortable:

> *I went out in the gusty dark*
> *To see how that long corpse would look,*
> *But had not thought the moon was whirling*
> *Mottled-white like a new shilling—*

The up-to-date note is struck here by the moon, but the
rest is easy and reassuring. It is probably not necessary to
exhibit another infidelity to beauty, the short poem "The
Sepulcher," which acknowledges the existence of the later
Yeats.

In *Darkling Plain* Miss Sara Bard Field brings us some
of the enthusiasm and exuberant metaphor that persons
like myself, ignorant of the Far West, usually associate

with that fabulous region. But first of all in a "Note to Fellow Marxists" she warns them not to reach too deeply into the true doctrine when they are writing verse, lest the very depth of emotion stirred by the Cause make for bad poetry. Miss Field reports a theory, passed on to her by Mr. John Cowper Powys, which she summarizes:

If composition takes place on the first and highest [plane], it will be superficial; if on the third and lowest, it will be self-involved. If, however, the intensity of the lowest stratum meets the detachment of the highest on a middle plane, a poem may be born.

I do not know whether Mr. Powys is responsible for the imagery here, but it is a kind of poem itself, for the idea of a poem's being born seems to me very nice. Mr. Powys gave Miss Field the theory in response to a poem that she had sent him, a poem "about an agonizing, pivotal personal experience." I do not know whether any of the poems in this book are like that, and while I should not like to think Miss Field "superficial," the high, sustained soprano of her performance indicates constant occupation of the "first and highest" plane; or is the highest plane still higher? Or do I misunderstand the theory? Here are some lines to Elinor Wylie:

> *Bright loveliness like cloisonné enamel*
> *Concealed a silver purpose so austere,*
> *So spherical of vision it could trammel*
> *Its fair, ephemeral coverture to clear*

Unhampered way for art's proud equipages
To roll beyond her hour and bear her thought,
Yet in those regal gifts despatched to ages
Her beauty, ashes now, is also caught.

Miss Field invites constant rereading, and I am sure that
her constant reader will agree with me that what she writes
could hardly be better done.

Mr. C. F. MacIntyre is resourceful, and his book brings
together intelligently, but I think not for any strong purpose of his own, certain influences that were fashionable
in the last decade. I do not mean that these influences are
not still good—we shall see that Mr. Blackmur uses them to
great advantage—yet it is plain that Mr. MacIntyre's facility is so omnivorous that he can take in Crane, Pound,
Cummings, Eliot, and Ransom, and give them all back
before he has discovered their relation to an intention of
his own. There is not a poem in this volume that is quite
all bad; but there is none entirely good. Mr. MacIntyre's
first difficulty seems to me to exist for him prior to any
considerations of style and prosody: his mind is stocked
with phrases from the past and they get in his way. The
ending of the poem, "For My Sister," his most successful
piece of composition, is ruined by an echo from one of
Shakespeare's sonnets:

She lives now, white in my mind, in a garland of leaves,
quick yet as dawn pitched up by the moon's thin horn:
a hill-top wisp not time's fell whip can tame,
the wraith of my sister who was never born.

It profits Mr. MacIntyre but little to change Shakespeare's "hand" to "whip": the insistence of the echo kept him from completing the image of the "wisp," and the line becomes further muddled by "tame," which is obviously there as a rhyme, remotely delayed, for "flame" and "name," six or seven lines back; but the rhyme being free and "organic," the need for it was not compelling, since there was no pattern to be completed.

This habit of using a phrase for its own sake, whether his own or somebody else's, tends to make all of Mr. MacIntyre's poems sound alike—in spite of the frequent brilliant lines. Put into terms of immediate effect, the fault may be seen as one of composition; but the defect is probably more fundamental. There is seldom a reason why these poems should not be either longer or shorter than they are. The interesting "Remanded"—interesting in spite of the "influence" behind it, an influence that dominates the poem not merely in certain rhythms but even in the syntax—would be better for the absence of the last stanza; but Mr. MacIntyre was evidently overwhelmed by one of his least pertinent images—

> *...and the roots*
> *call the pink-nippled buds home for a nap—*

and he wrote an eight-line stanza in order to use it. But in spite of this very distinct fault—and it is a fault of a somewhat prodigal gift for language—Mr. MacIntyre ought to be in his next book one of the good poets of the 'thirties if

he can define for himself a little better what he wants to
do.

If Mr. MacIntyre's trouble is a certain bewilderment
amid so many phases of the period style of his elders, Mr.
Lawrence Lee has, up to the present volume, *Monticello
and Other Poems,* paid too little attention to the innovations in language made by his immediate predecessors. I
should not suggest that these innovations are valuable in
themselves. Mr. Yeats, since about 1910, has made for himself a new poetic speech, but apart from what he conveys
with it—if it were possible to consider it apart—his style
is very close to some ideal of ordinary, educated speech:
his immense originality consists in the peculiar kind of
meaning, in a special vision of the world, that this "ordinary" language is made to create. That is one way of making innovations of language in poetry. In Mr. Lee's new
book there are still traces of his earlier manner, and I
select at random this beginning of a sonnet called "Days
like Buttercups":

> *Hardly the grass has come and they are there,*
> *Suddenly shaking a yellow in the rain,*
> *Starring the green earth and the rain-washed air*
> *Like gathered dreams of childhood sprung again.*

This is merely inoffensive, and it is not, as it is supposed
to be by our popular critics, the central tradition of style.
It is definitely a period style, 1900 to 1914. But throughout
the book one finds moments of another sort of style, and

doubtless Mr. Lee in his next book will tune his whole style to them, and not leave them scattered and almost accidental:

> *The wind filled all dark outside with cold sound*
> *And rattled the windows of our house.*

And this, from the title-poem:

> *We shall not have from seasons peace, nor know*
> *Comfort in red leaves shaking.*

I do not know whether Mr. Lee wrote these two passages with difficulty, but I surmise that a style based upon the very special rhythm and vowel sounds would give him or any other poet a hard time. Most of Mr. Lee's work is too easy for him, and it is my guess that greater technical stringency would lead him to important discoveries in sensibility and thought.

Miss Louise Bogan has published three books, and with each book she has been getting a little better, until now, in the three or four best poems of *The Sleeping Fury*, she has no superior within her purpose and range: among the women poets of our time she has a single peer, Miss Léonie Adams. Neither Miss Bogan nor Miss Adams will ever have the popular following of Miss Millay or even of the late Elinor Wylie. I do not mean to detract from these older poets; they are technically proficient, they are serious, and they deserve the kind of reputations they have won. Miss Bogan and Miss Adams deserve still greater reputations, but they will not get them in our time because they are "purer" poets than Miss Millay and Mrs. Wylie. They are purer because their work is less involved in the moral and stylistic fashions of the age, and they efface themselves. Miss Millay never lets us forget her "advanced" point of view, nor Mrs. Wylie her interesting personality.

In addition to distinguished diction and a fine ear for the phrase-rhythm, Miss Bogan has mastered a prosody that permits her to get the greatest effect out of the slightest variation of stress.

> *In the cold heart, as on a page,*
> *Spell out the gentle syllable*
> *That puts short limit to your rage*
> *And curdles the straight fire of hell,*
> *Compassing all, so all is well.*

There is nothing flashy about it; it is finely modulated; and I think one needs only to contrast Miss Bogan's control of imagery in this stanza, the toning down of the metaphor to the direct last line, with the metaphorical juggernaut to which Miss Field's muse has tied herself, to see the fundamental difference between mastery of an artistic medium and mere undisciplined talent. Miss Bogan is at her best in "Henceforth, from the Mind," surely one of the finest lyrics of our time. The "idea" of the poem is the gradual fading away of earthly joy upon the approach of age—one of the stock themes of English poetry;

and Miss Bogan presents it with all the freshness of an Elizabethan lyricist. I quote the two last stanzas:

> *Henceforth, from the shell,*
> *Wherein you heard, and wondered*
> *At oceans like a bell*
> *So far from ocean sundered—*
> *A smothered sound that sleeps*
> *Long lost within lost deeps,*
>
> *Will chime you change and hours,*
> *The shadow of increase,*
> *Will sound you flowers,*
> *Born under troubled peace—*
> *Henceforth, henceforth*
> *Will echo sea and earth.*

This poem represents the best phase of Miss Bogan's work: it goes back to an early piece that has been neglected by readers and reviewers alike—"The Mark"—and these two poems would alone entitle Miss Bogan to the consideration of the coming age.

But there is an unsatisfactory side to Miss Bogan's verse, and it may be briefly indicated by pointing out that the peculiar merits of "The Mark" and "Henceforth, from the Mind" seem to lie in a strict observance of certain limitations: in these poems and, of course, in others, Miss Bogan is impersonal and dramatic. In "The Sleeping Fury" she is philosophical and divinatory; in "Hypocrite

Swift" she merely adumbrates an obscure dramatic situation in a half-lyrical, half-eighteenth-century, satirical style. Neither of these poems is successful, and the failure can be traced to all levels of the performances; for example, to the prosody, which has little relation to the development of the matter and which merely offers us a few clever local effects.

I have postponed consideration of Mr. Blackmur to the last, because with the publication of *From Jordan's Delight* we may see for the first time the capacity and range of one of the best American poets. It is to be expected from the critical conscience that Mr. Blackmur applies to his contemporaries, that he should exercise it upon himself. He is no longer, I suppose, a "young writer," yet surely some of these poems were written years ago and perhaps rewritten many times before their inclusion here. Blackmur could have published a volume of verse ten years ago: I infer that he has waited until he could meet the severe standards that he has demanded of others, in *The Double Agent,* which is the best technical criticism of poetry by an American since *The Sacred Wood.*

Although Blackmur has been influenced by Stevens and Eliot, and even by Cummings and Hart Crane, his style is in no sense a period style, and is definitely his own. Echoes of his contemporaries appear chiefly in poems that are otherwise his least interesting work. The two impressive series of poems, "From Jordan's Delight" and "Sea Island Miscellany," contain none of these impurities, or if they do, they have been used so well that they are not easily detected. More positively Blackmur's style invites the technical criticism of which he has been so distinguished a practitioner: he is a poet with a compelling sense of form, and a considerable achievement of form spares us the speculative task of "obscure metaphysical reflection."

In the excellent piece called "The Spear," which is poem III of a series entitled "Dedications," there is a passage that I quote both for its substance, which is a kind of artistic credo, and for its style:

> *Leave me my Odyssey,*
> *the living soul's hyperbole,*
> *peril in which to hide,*
> *peace for my naked eyes.*
> *O let my heart*
> *that spurns satieties*
> *be living hooked from the fresh flood*
> *but let my soul rehearse*
> *without benefit or curse*
> *of a saviour's blood*
> *its difficult and dangerous art.*

Earlier in the poem there is the statement,

> *Salvation is a salmon speared,*
> *the ancient Fisher cried.*

The spear of salvation may wait until death, and meanwhile without benefit of a supernatural religion, or in terms of Mr. Blackmur's immediate problem as a poet, without benefit of a "ready-made mould" of ideas, a structure of imaginative reference, he will practice the art of poetry. As to the style of this passage, it is sufficient to remark here that several of the terms are replaceable. The "Odyssey" is possibly the adventure of the discoverer of experience, but it is an allusion, not an objective reference. Likewise "soul" is interchangeable with *mind* or *imagination*—which appreciably weakens the force of "hyperbole," and, in the line "but let my soul rehearse," is too weak to inform the action of the verb. So, here in this brief creed of the poet, we are at a loss to know what the foundation of his procedure is: fortunately he offers us other evidence—in addition to his concrete achievement, which is the best evidence—of the integrity of his purposes.

The interesting sequence of four sonnets, called "Judas Priest," "discusses" the relation of the artist to experience: the relation is simply that of Judas to the Passion of our Lord. I quote sonnet III:

> *Judas, not Pilate, had a wakened mind*
> *and knew what agony must come about;*
> *while Pilate washed his hands of all mankind,*
> *he saw necessity past Pilate's doubt.*
>
> *So driven mad did he alone indict*
> *the waste the terror the intolerable loss,*
> *the near abyss of darkness in the light,*
> *and made a live tree of a wooden cross.*

Where then are we?—we lookers-on of art,
outsiders by tormented wilful choice,
condemned to image death in each live heart,
and kiss it so—and how shall we rejoice?
   But if men prophesy Gethsemane
   Regardless, there must some regard the tree.

I have not quoted this as an example of Blackmur's best work, but rather as a focus of some of his limitations, which if clearly grasped will illuminate the essential properties of the eight or ten distinguished poems in this volume. Although Blackmur, in sonnet IV, addresses the Communists as "comrades of a simpler faith," and thus places his conception of the artist not only against the background of the Passion but also in terms of a contemporary "cause," he nevertheless seems to insist upon the quite simple distinction between action and observation as the basis of his work. The poet is not an indifferent Pilate; he is the Judas who betrays, in the sense of remaining aloof from, action.

As I shall indicate in a moment, observation is not the exact word for Blackmur's conception of the role of the poet. I have used it in a preliminary distinction, in order to make the comment that all such distinctions, action versus contemplation, morals versus art, are in themselves neither sound nor unsound: a poet who eschews the inculcation of moral precepts may nevertheless be a morally sound poet, and a poet who exhorts, like Mr. John Holmes, may have little or no moral value. The tests of the distinction as Blackmur apprehends it must be found in his best verse.

Before we proceed to that, I shall seem again a little ungrateful to Mr. Blackmur in pointing out in the quoted sonnet defects similar to those in "The Spear." The sonnet is Shakespearean in form: three quatrains developing serially towards the synthesis of the couplet; at the ninth line begins the "application" of the matter set forth in the two first quatrains, so that we get—what Shakespeare seldom used—an octet followed by quatrain-and-couplet so arranged as to imitate the effect of a genuine sestet; the couplet is detached grammatically but because it must complete the sense of the inconclusive twelfth line, it forms with the third quatrain a unit. Altogether this is as nice a piece of sonnet technique as you will find in modern verse; and the versification seems to me excellent. But there is something unsatisfactory in its total effect, and I think we may get at the difficulty through a brief analysis of "necessity" in line four, of the whole of line eight, and of the play upon "regardless" and "regard" in the last line.

Why did Judas see "necessity" instead of an image—which would have been Yeats's way of dramatizing the "scene"? Blackmur gives us an uninformed and unsupported abstraction—as he does in the first of these four sonnets: "that watch new *bloodshed* waste god's death again." The second quatrain accumulates a series of rhetorical anti-images towards a climax which is thus not prepared for: the antithesis of tree and cross cuts off one's attention from the "scene" of the octet and is, in effect, the beginning of a core of meaning that, because the sonnet-structure demands it, is suddenly dropped. In the fourteenth line "regardless" means something like "without looking," "without care for the qualities inherent in the situation"; "regard" thus means "look at for its particular qualities." But the shock of the paranomasia here also is the beginning of a new "meaning," for the precision of the word-play exists on the purely logical, and not on the imaginative and synthesizing, plane.

This has been a long way round to a simple statement— and I have taken the long way because Blackmur is a poet who raises the fundamental problems of his art; he cannot be fixed in a generalization without one's previously showing how one has arrived at it. That simple statement is: Blackmur writes from two different *points d'appui,* the one abstract, the other immediate and dramatic. We have looked at the detail of two of his abstractly motivated poems, and the conclusion seems inevitable: that he takes the "idea" and then tries to reduce it to image, with the result that the images do not always materialize out of the idea. Of course, a merely logical reversal of this method would not remedy the trouble; but to state it so, on the bare logical basis, is enough I think to indicate the kind of defect that renders unsound this phase of Blackmur's work. Blackmur as a critic is a master of ideas, but as a poet he is occasionally mastered by them. This does not mean that the "idea" of sonnet III of "Judas Priest," as a critical analysis of the function of poetry in relation to

action, is unsound; it is rather that the idea is not available
to Blackmur on the level of poetry. And this limitation
witnesses again the difficulty of our age in writing philosophical poetry—a poetry springing from an apprehension,
however profound, of ideas.

The distinction that I have just labored will, I hope,
cast into relief the perfection of achievement in the bulk
of Blackmur's poetry. I cannot do better than to quote
one of the perfect lyrics (it is number IX of "Sea Island
Miscellany"), entitled "Mirage":

> *The wind was in another country, and*
> *the day had gathered to its heart of noon*
> *the sum of silence, heat, and stricken time.*
> *Not a ripple spread. The sea mirrored*
> *perfectly all the nothing in the sky.*
> *We had to walk about to keep our eyes*
> *from seeing nothing, and our hearts from stopping*
> *at nothing. Then most suddenly we saw*
> *horizon on horizon lifting up*
> *out of the sea's edge a shining mountain*
> *sun-yellow and sea-green; against it surf*
> *flung spray and spume into the miles of sky.*
> *Somebody said mirage, and it was gone,*
> *but there I have been living ever since.*

As an historical reference for the poem I suppose the word
symbolism is enough to indicate the sensibility and technique. The "human situation" is clearer than Mallarmé

would have made it; the landscape is a little more toned down than Rimbaud would have liked; but it is definitely a symbolist poem.

Although it seems to me perfect of its kind—examine the adjectives in the fourth from the last line and the use of "miles" in the next line—it is not quite typical of Blackmur's best: I have quoted it to establish the extreme limit of his sensibility and so to point out that, at his best, his poetry arrives at form in terms of the implicit relation of a sensuous complex to the inherent order of his mind. And this method is precisely the opposite of the abstract procedure that I have analyzed in "The Spear" and in the sonnet from "Judas Priest." Number V of "Sea Island Miscellany" will show the method that Blackmur uses in his most characteristic poems:

> *One grey and foaming day*
> *I looked from my lee shore*
> *landwards and across the bay:*
> *my eyes grew small and sore.*
>
> *Low in the low sea-waves*
> *the coast-line sank from sight;*
> *the viewless, full sea-graves*
> *stood open like the night:*
>
> *(sea waters are most bare*
> *when darkness spreads her trawl,*
> *the sea-night winds her snare*
> *either for ship or soul).*

Once along this coast
my fathers made their sail
and were with all hands lost,
outweathered in a gale.

Now from long looking I
have come on second sight,
there where the lost shores lie
the sea is breeding night.

As in this poem, so in the most interesting work in this
book, Blackmur's imagery is derived from observation of
an island off the coast of Maine, Jordan's Delight: it is
more than imagery derived; the sea is here the symbol of
the treachery of nature constantly challenging the moral
resources of civilized man. This conflict, conceived not
abstractly but dramatically, in terms of experience, is the
substance of a poetry as sound as any that has been written
in our time. On another occasion it may be proper to
connect it with a wider historical background, and to look
into its significance as a special quality of the romantic
sensibility. It is a poetry that combines the richness of
perception and the apparent release to the flux of experience, usually found in the romantic poets, with rigorous
form and implicit intellectual order.

THE FUNCTION OF THE
CRITICAL QUARTERLY

I F THE quarterly journal has ceased forever to be our popular magazine, may it still be said that the specialized critical quarterly has a "use"? *Use* is a term too slippery to invite definition. Since the time I became aware of the literary magazine, nearly twenty years ago, the declining usefulness of the critical quarterly has been taken for granted. It now increasingly serves the end of acquainting unpopular writers with one another's writings. That is a "use" that I, for one, am not prepared to deride. But the reader is entitled to his own sense of usefulness. He is the cultivated layman who felt at one time, say a hundred years ago, that the high places of literature were not beyond his reach: he saw himself and the author in a communion of understanding in which the communicants were necessary to each other.

It is a communion lost to us. The weekly and the monthly, renovated for modern speed of the eye, have captured the intelligent layman entirely.[1] And for a good reason. At his best he likes his "theory," as he educatedly names ideas, mixed unobtrusively into the "practice" of

[1] Since this was written, *Life, Look, Pic, Click,* and other picture magazines have appeared.

his times: he likes to believe that the literary news of his period can bring him a sufficient criticism of it. And this was precisely what was procured for him, at a high level of excellence, by the British quarterlies in the day of Lockhart, Jeffrey, and Wilson. The layman found out what was happening at the same time that he was told what it meant.

Doubtless our own splitting off of information from understanding, this modern divorce of action from intelligence, is general, and not particular to the arts of literature. If it is a problem that on every hand confronts us, it must affect the policy of the critical review—and tremendously determine it. For the critical review stands for one-half of the modern dilemma, the purer half: the intelligence trying to think into the moving world a rational order of value.

The critical review then must severely define its relation first to a public and then to its contributors. The editor's attitude towards his contributors, his choice of contributors, and his direction of their work, depend upon the kind of influence that he has decided to exercise.

Our best quarterlies have readers but not enough readers to pay the "cost of production." The quarterly must be subsidized; it either runs on a subsidy or does not run. It cannot define its "use" in terms of the size of its public; and it assumes that the public needs something that it does not want, or—what is the same thing—that a minority wants what the greater public needs. The leading quarterlies are subsidized by universities or are backed, like the late *Hound and Horn,* by persons whose fortunes and interests may be expected to change. The fate of *The Symposium,* the best critical quarterly published in America up to its time (1929-1933), offers timely warning to the founder of a review that cannot count upon a subsidy or a private fortune.

There is no record of success for a quarterly review that, in recent times, has tried to compete with the weekly or the monthly. The weekly reader gets the news of books and affairs while it is still, I imagine, hot; and if he longs for a little meditation upon the moving shadows on the wall of the cave, he will take not much more of this than he can get out of the pages of the monthly—regretting that the meditation is a month old and that something new to be meditated upon has, last week or yesterday, risen to invalidate the old meditation. Of course we ought to enjoin the reader to suspect the monthly meditation; it was perhaps not sufficiently considered and fundamental. We ought, in fact, to tell him that the critical quarterly, devoted to principles, can alone give him a meditation of such considered depth that it will illuminate the risen event of yesterday, or the rising event of tomorrow. But unfortunately the modern reader's synthesizing powers are limited, and nothing is applicable to nothing, and the gap between idea and event leaves the reader and the quarterly somewhat high and dry with respect to each other. The quarterly is always too late, even if its standards are not stubbornly too high. If the quarterly imitates the freshness of the weekly, its freshness is necessarily three months stale, refrigerated but not new; and if it tries for the liveliness of monthly commentary, its peril is the sacrifice of leisured thought. In either instance the quarterly sacrifices its standards only to attempt a work that it cannot hope to do.

But if the quarterly editor is not forced by poverty to run a monthly *manqué*, his problem at once becomes simpler and more difficult; simpler, because he does not need to find out by trial and error what a paying public will read; more difficult, because he must become himself a first-rate critic in the act of organizing his material, four times a year, into coherent criticism.

The critical performance of the quarterly lies no more in the critical essays than in the "creative" department; fine creative work is a criticism of the second rate; and the critical department ought to be run for the protection of that which in itself is the end of criticism. If this observation be extended to society and social criticism, the complete function of the quarterly will emerge. For only the social criticism that instances the value of concrete social experience may be termed properly critical. Literature in this broadest sense tells us the meaning of experience, what it is and has been, and it is there that the political and aesthetic departments join.

It is a formidable union, and the difficulty of consummating it may well appall the stoutest editorial heart. Given the freedom to engage the difficulty, the editor is immediately assailed by a series of questions. Is there a critical task that might be done effectively by the quarterly? Can it be done at the present time? If it can, how can it best be done?

Though it would be untrue to say that good critical essays never appear in the monthly magazines, yet an effective critical program cannot, in that medium, be maintained. The monthly is too close to the weekly, the weekly to the newspaper, for any of these kinds of organ to maintain a critical program in the midst of the more pressing need to report the "scene." If one use of criticism is to make the reader aware of himself through the literature of his time, and aware, through this literature, of the literature of the past, the critical program must have an objective, and not be contented with partial glimpses or mere reports of points of view. The reader needs more than the mere news that a given point of view exists; he must be initiated into the point of view, saturated with it. The critical program must, then, supply its readers with coherent standards of taste and examples of taste in operation; not mere statements about taste. Mere reporting enjoins the editor to glance at all points of view. The reader gets a "digest" of opinion, not critical thought; and he is encouraged to sample everything and to experience nothing.

A sound critical program has at least this one feature: *it allows to the reader no choice in the standards of judgment.* It asks the reader to take a post of observation, and to occupy it long enough to examine closely the field before him, which is presumably the whole field of our experience. This, one supposes, is dogmatism, but it is arguable still that dogma in criticism is a permanent necessity: the value of the dogma will be determined by the quality of the mind engaged in constructing it. For dogma is coherent thought in the pursuit of principles. If the critic has risen to the plane of principle, and refuses to judge by prejudice, he will, while allowing no quarter to critical relativity, grant enormous variety to the specific arts. For it must be remembered that prejudice is not dogma, that the one has no toleration of the other. If prejudice were dogma, the *New York Times Book Review* would be a first-rate critical organ. It allows the narrowest possible range of artistic performance along with the widest latitude of incoherent opinion—simply because it uses, instead of principle, prejudice.

To deny the use of the critical quarterly today is to deny the use of criticism. It is a perilous denial. For criticism is not merely a way of saying that a certain poem is better than another; it gives meaning to the awareness of differences only in so far as it instructs the reader in three fundamentals of mounting importance: the exercise of taste, the pursuit of standards of intellectual judgment, and the acquisition of self-knowledge. If the reader is not encouraged in self-knowledge—a kind of knowing that entails insight into one's relation to a moral and social order that one has begun, after great labor, to understand—then taste and judgment have no center, and are mere words.

If this is the task of criticism, and if the task of criticism can be accomplished only in the quarterly, what is to prevent its being carried out? There are obstacles. To distinguish cause and effect is neither easy nor, fortunately, obligatory: living evidence of the divorce of fact and understanding, of action and intelligence, is the mass-produced monthly. It is a kind of journalism that includes both the Hearst magazines and the "quality" group. The Hearst readers have always existed potentially; the "quality" readers number in their ranks many new recruits, but quite as many must surely be persons with an education that formerly qualified them to read the critical quarterly. Such readers have a certain sensibility, but not being actively critical themselves, they take what comes; and the monthly magazine, being efficiently because profitably distributed, is what they take. The inference to be studied here, if the inference were not already visible as fact, is that the quarterly must be heavily subsidized.

There is still another obstacle to successful quarterly publication: the task of getting suitable contributors. Or perhaps the obstacle is the effect of the monthly magazine on writers who might, but for its existence, be constantly available to the quarterly editor. The quality group, for example, can pay better rates for manuscripts than the most flourishing quarterly can ever pay. The monthly can command first choice of the work of writers who would otherwise put their best effort into the more considered, and to them more satisfactory, performance demanded by the more critical journal. If the quarterly pay five dollars a page, critics trying to set forth a program, and "creative" writers who wish to exhibit their work in terms of the coherent standards of those critics, will accept the five dollars a page—provided the lure of a bigger price does not meanwhile keep them from doing their better and more serious work. The menacing possibility of eight or ten dollars a page is, by writers of all sorts, gratefully embraced. The writer is offering a commodity for sale, and he, like every other producer, must get the highest price.

It is a law of "capitalism." There is no moral theory that can place a stigma upon this procedure. If it were possible for good writers deliberately to lower their quality, that would be a horse of another color; but the leveling comes from the market itself, which asks for a superficial, fragmentary performance that may, within the assigned limits, be excellent work. In the long run it is futile work, because it cannot be systematic and comprehensive. The writer, if he happen to be a critic, must begin his program over again with every essay, and journalize his thought out of existence: he cannot develop continuity of thought because he cannot count upon the attention of the same readers over a number of years: he is selling on the open market, and he cannot be sure that his product will be bought by the same *entrepreneur* a second time. He fidgets in this insecure, chaotic position because he must—or starve—seek the highest money reward for his work.

If the quarterly shall be less fragmentary than the monthly, it must maintain a policy that not only demands the leisured, considered performance; it has got to make the performance possible to its contributors. I suggest that

the quarterly pay the highest rate it can—cheapening perhaps the quality of its paper and printing—but not that
it try to compete in prices with the monthly. There is, I
think, a compromise. And the compromise, a concession
to the writer and an eventual benefit to the editor, consists in breaking the law of capitalism already referred to.
One article of this law grows out of the merely cash nexus
between the producer and the distributor—between writer
and editor—and it urges the distributor to be as disloyal
as possible—for a purpose—to the producer of the commodity which he sells. The distributor's purpose is to keep
the producer insecure and humble, so that, should the
strain of competition permit, he can give the producer the
lowest possible price. For here it may be said that the
monthly pays a better price than the quarterly, not because
it is by good luck more prosperous and by nature more
generous, but because competition forces it to pay ten
dollars a page for work that might go to another editor
for nine.

The quarterly must be loyal to its contributors in two
indispensable ways, and both these ways involve another
kind of "nexus" between writer and editor than the cash.
A genuine critical objective cannot be attained if the editor waits on the market for what may arrive in the mail.
If he has a mind, he must make up his mind what he
wants, and decide that there are certain contributors whom
he would rather have than others. There will be perhaps
a dozen of these and the editor has got to be loyal to them.
If he is a second-rate man, and fears that, by giving rein

over a long stretch to a talented group of men, he will be personally overshadowed, he had better write the entire contents of his magazine—a feat that, being a second-rate man, he will not be equal to.

Whether he be first- or second-rate, his first proof of loyalty is the highest price that he can pay. If the editor wants to enlist a regular staff of contributors whom he can call upon at a moment's notice, he should pay them a little more than he will pay for the casual manuscript, however good, that he found on his desk this morning. Authors are as responsive to kind treatment as other labor. They will feel for this editor a corresponding loyalty. They will let him have for five dollars a page, for instance, a manuscript that, after a little blood-letting, they might easily sell for ten to a quality magazine. They will do this all the more eagerly if the editor is willing to let the writer continue the work in three or four more essays, or stories, or poems; if, in short, the writers are encouraged in their programs.

That, in fact, is the editor's second loyalty—to take most of the output of his selected, inner circle of contributors. He must assume, if he does not actually know, that his contributors are not men of independent income. He must take a responsible view of their welfare. If he does not, the lure of high prices will attract their work into the open market. If the quarterly editor's attitude is indistinguishable from that of the commercial magazine, he is doomed to fail.

For, let his literary standards be the highest, his relation to his contributors is still commercial, even if he is not trying "to make money." He is only a less effective part of a system that the writer cannot afford to be loyal to. Both the serious writer and the critical quarterly are thus defeated. I could name a dozen leading writers, north and south, who remember the quarterlies for manuscripts that they cannot sell elsewhere at high prices. The quarterly review gets what is left in the trunk.

There is no use blinking these facts. It is futile to discuss the higher aims of the critical review without facing them. There is, of course, a very small group of writers— the present writer is doubtless one of them—whose aims are directed towards the limited audience of the critical review. It is not an exalted purpose that so confines them; it is only the accident of concentration. If the quarterly editor's attitude is the same as his commercial colleague's, the performance of his critical minority is not more effective than the scattered performance of the hack writer seeking the open market. The minority suffers the restriction of audience without enjoying the satisfaction of taking part in a literature, and without getting the higher pay of competition.

Given the right relation between the editor and his contributors, what work may they together be expected to do? The question is rhetorical; but I think it is clear that nothing useful can be done without that right relation. Modern experiments in quarterly publication achieve moderate success; they win readers, a very few, year after year. The best quarterlies indirectly affect the "quality" reader, for the "quality" writer is often formed by the quarterly that his public never sees. But the quarterly that would justify the name of criticism must have a set purpose—not merely to publish the "best" that drifts into its office; its internal organization and its outward policy must be sharply defined.

The great magazines have been edited by autocrats. Within the memory of our time the great editors were Henley and Ford; in our own age, the late A. R. Orage and T. S. Eliot. Ford Madox Ford had notable success with *The English Review,* as early as 1909, because he knew what men to bring to the front: he gave concentration of purpose, the conviction of being part of a literature, to at least half of the distinguished writers who survived the War and who have deeply influenced our own age. He, more than any other modern editor, enrolled his contributors in the profession of letters—in a time when, under finance-capitalism, editors had already become employers who felt as little responsibility to their labor as manufacturers are able to feel towards theirs.

The Criterion under T. S. Eliot has been the best quarterly of our time.[2] It has become the fashion to deride it: its intellectualism, its traditionalism, its devotion to "lost causes," expose it to an attack that for my purpose here need not be discussed. The value of its critical program does not concern me at the moment. It has been important because it does have a critical program: the editor from the beginning set out to develop critical issues. For a

[2] It suspended publication with the January 1939 issue.

brief period, around 1926 or 1927, *The Criterion* became
a monthly; it soon reverted to quarterly appearance. In
the reduced size of the monthly the editor could not print
contributions long enough to carry considered critical discussion.

If the task of the quarterly is to impose an intelligible
order upon a scattering experience that the monthly and
the weekly may hope only to report, the task of the editor
must be one of difficulty and responsibility. We must expect him to have power and influence. His power should
be concentrated if—it is worth repeating again—he is not
merely to do what the monthly can do better. There can
be little doubt that the success of *The Criterion*—it has
never, I believe, had more than two thousand subscribers
—has been due to concentrated editorship functioning
through a small group of regular contributors. By group
I do not mean the personal friends of the editor, or persons enlisted in some movement, for a movement is not
always a program. By a group I mean a number of writers
who agree that certain fundamental issues exist and who
consent, under direction of the editor, to discuss them
with a certain emphasis. The editor may not believe in
Marxism or neo-Thomism, but he will see it as an issue,
and he will seek discussion of Marxism or neo-Thomism
from a point of view.

I have described the high aims of the critical quarterly
as if financial backing were not a problem; as if the editor
were at liberty to develop his program unhampered by
the need of cash subscribers; as if his magazine were free

to find whatever public may exist for it. All writing seeks an audience. But the editor has a responsibility that he must discharge as perfectly as the contingencies of backing and public will permit. He owes his first duty to his critical principles, his sense of the moral and intellectual order upon which society ought to rest, whether or not society at the moment has an interest in such an order or is even aware of a need for it. For the ideal task of the critical quarterly is not to give the public what it wants, or what it thinks it wants, but what—through the medium of its most intelligent members—it ought to have. At a time when action has become singularly devoid of intelligence, there could not be a "cause" more disinterested. The way to give the public what it resentfully needs is to discredit the inferior ideas of the age by exposing them to the criticism of the superior ideas.

LIBERALISM AND TRADITION

I

MODERN CONTROVERSIALISTS appeal, at some stage in the discussion, to two related questions that are, in a pragmatic age, two ways of seeing the same problem. A critic asks his opponent: Is your program practicable? If the critic decides that the program will work, he does not ask the second question, but he is certain to ask it if he thinks that the scheme of his opponent has no chance of "success": What in the first place is the basis of your belief in this program?

The two questions are necessarily the same in the moral climate of positivism in which we live. I have no objection to the identification. It is only necessary that we should know what we are talking about. The validity of my belief in my ability to walk across the street depends strictly upon the pragmatic test. But that is not the kind of belief that we are pointing to when we say: Chastity is a good; politics is philosophically "above" economics; man partakes of the divine nature. By the pragmatic test it can be shown that the negatives of these beliefs can be made in some sense to "work."

But that does not disqualify the beliefs. From the moral,

but not the positivist, point of view, the value of the "working" is the degree to which it realizes the belief: the standard invoked here attributes greater reality to the objective than to the process. To the positivist there is only process. Let us glance at an example of "objective" wherein the "process" is wholly absorbed into its terms. Mr. Jones announces: "I have achieved a spiritual regeneration." He has isolated an experience in terms of a belief, which thus gains a sensible, concrete body. The experience exists in terms of the belief.

Take Mr. Jones's regeneration another way. Let a social psychologist look at him and say: "Mr. Jones has achieved a better adjustment to his environment." The psychologist has isolated the experience, which he calls the "behavior," of Mr. Jones in an entirely new set of terms that omit the belief that poor Jones thought he was acting upon. The psychologist substitutes for Jones's "rationalization" an inference built up upon an experimental observation of his behavior. What Jones did, not what he thought he was doing, was his real belief. Jones's own procedure has been completely reversed by the psychologist. His belief has been absorbed by his behavior—his objective absorbed by a process.

II

Now the next step of the positivist critic: there is, he says, no argument here—you believe one thing, I another. Even if I wanted to believe in your program, the assumption of my thought would not let me. Based upon your assumptions are many beliefs that I find interesting and even desirable, but I cannot go all the way with you because not only will the ground of my beliefs hinder me; the very fact that nine men out of ten today share my view makes your program extremely doubtful of success. We are committed to a view in which your beliefs have little or no efficacy; we are committed to a program of our own that, in spite of its defects, has dominated the modern world. For good or ill we must make the best of it.

This state of mind is Liberalism. It is the attitude of Mr. Dudley Wynn, whose essay in the January, 1936, number of *The Virginia Quarterly Review* will reward the reader's closest attention. Mr. Wynn makes out—accidentally, I take it—a powerful case for tradition as he understands it. He finds "tradition" attractive, but he cannot believe in it. He can believe in Liberalism. He says:

If one accepts the views of the Agrarians, one accepts them; if one cannot accept those views, one can only try to show the points at which belief balks. It is not a question of what one feels one needs to believe, but simply of what one can believe.

Liberals from William James to Walter Lippmann and Mr. Wynn, constantly stress the *can*—the possibility of certain beliefs. One must agree with them that there are legitimate and illegitimate objects of belief, but evidently Mr. Wynn and other Liberals have made up their minds

to swallow everything or to starve to death: we must believe everything or nothing. The dilemma is historically
the most naïve feature of the whole positivist movement.
Positivism thinks that it does not *believe;* it rigorously
proves.

But Mr. Wynn is not an enthusiastic Liberal; he is
rather a disappointed traditionist. He is for tradition, and
I think it is fair to say that he is against Liberalism. Yet
he is vehemently against traditionists, and in favor of Liberals. That is to say, he sympathizes with the necessary
unbelief of the modern Liberal. Tradition is good, but
persons who believe in it must be deluding themselves,
and he is against them.

Let us see definitely what he is against, for what Mr.
Wynn opposes is what a great many Liberals balk at—
because they can believe only what it is possible to believe.
For example: the Liberal will not accept what has lately
been known as the Agrarian economics because, according
to Mr. Wynn, it involves belief in religious authority. It
is not possible today to believe in religious authority. The
syllogism concealed here is unexceptionable, but its logic
was used on another occasion to make the Mad Hatter's
tea party one of the memorable scenes in literature. For
Mr. Wynn deduces the Agrarian belief in religious authority in the following manner:

First, Tate wrote an essay called "Religion and the Old
South," in which he pointed out two things—that the "pro-
gressivist" view of history is the relativist view in which
the religious absolute disintegrates, and that wicked view

rose upon the debris of medieval Catholicism, which stood for religious authority; therefore since Tate is an Agrarian, an anti-modernist who deplores the relativist view, he must necessarily believe in religious authority. And if the other Agrarians were only rigorous enough, they would see the implications of their position, and believe in it too.

Secondly, the English Distributists believe in the value of agriculture and small ownership; the Agrarians believe in agriculture and small ownership. The English Distributists believe in monarchy and Catholicism; *therefore,* the Agrarians believe in monarchy and Catholicism.

I do not wish to be discourteous to a conscientious critic; but if this kind of logic is possible, then anything is possible; and I am at a loss to understand why Mr. Wynn cannot believe in so simple a thing as religious authority.

I do not believe in it, and it is my distinct impression that none of the writers called Agrarians has written a single sentence setting forth belief in it. *Neither the Agrarian economics nor religious authority is a legitimate object of belief, nor can it be.*

When Liberals say that belief in religious authority is impossible today, I reply that it is not only impossible today, it has always been impossible. No one has ever *believed* in it. I do not wish to labor the point: it is perhaps sufficient for the purpose to indicate that the Immaculate Conception, since it cannot be proved but only inferred to be either true or false, is a legitimate object of belief. Religious authority is not an object of belief; it is a matter of historical fact; it is the name for the exercise of a kind of authority that once existed in fact. Whether it shall exist again is speculative. And the foregoing argument is applicable to the so-called belief in the Agrarian, or any other, economics.

"It is not a question," says the Liberal, "of what one feels one needs to believe"—precisely. If I felt that I needed to believe in religious authority, I should commit suicide, for I should then be at liberty to feel that I needed to believe in thunder and roses. The Liberal mind —even when it leans towards tradition—has not been famous for its philosophical tact.

III

The problem of belief is not new. It harassed the Greeks, and the early Church Fathers were perfectly familiar with its modern implications. (It was not, then, invented by Mr. I. A. Richards.) The moral sophistication of Tertullian's *Credo quia absurdum* is a starting point for the modern dissociation of ideas. The Liberal sees the one idea as multiple, as a "series of progressively developing problems." But the Liberal, examining tradition, sets up his own idea of it and "dissociates" it as if it were somebody else's. Among these traditionist straw men is a monster who has been able to solve everything, because to him problems do not exist. The traditionist, for example, supposedly thinks that understanding is the equivalent of belief. If it were possible to believe in religious

authority and I wanted to believe in it, all I should have
to do would be to understand it historically. (Grant to the
traditionist an historical understanding of Catholicism: that
is a good enough pretext for the Liberal to tell the plain
citizen that the Agrarians want to put popery over on him
along with property.) Now the argument for the credulity
of the traditionist is this: the traditionist has "understood" the mentality of the thirteenth century; he thinks
that the world view of that century had features of great
value, of value more contributive to the dignity and total
welfare of men than the qualities of life available under
the world view of the twentieth century; therefore the
traditionist believes everything that the thirteenth century
believed.

There are doubtless traditionists who think they believe
all this, perhaps others who genuinely do believe it. If the
acceptance of all the beliefs of another age is a prerequisite
of traditionalism, I cannot qualify for it. I share with the
thirteenth century, or the eighteenth, or the twentieth, its
objects of belief neither through the descent of unbroken
generations nor by independent act of faith. I will be
explicit, and instance the particular situation. I am two
generations removed from Catholicism on the maternal
side of my family; on the paternal, I am removed at least
thirteen generations. But that does not, in my opinion,
prove anything about my eligibility to tradition.

Now a genuine religion commands us to consider absolutes. A man living in the stream of religious tradition
has the absolutes available to him; indeed, as Pascal main-

tained, he cannot evade them. But there are always the heretics on the one hand and, on the other, the apostates who combat the absolutes. The absolutes of religion, therefore, are not imperatives of belief; they are rather imperatives of reference. (Even in the science of psychology the Christian soul is still an imperative of reference, for the disintegrated, multiple "psyche" of modern man is intelligible only with reference to the historic unity of soul.) The dominating structure of a great civilized tradition is certain absolutes—points of moral and intellectual reference by which people live, and by which they must continue to live until in the slow crawl of history new references take their place. The "references" are never wholly new; medieval Europe itself was a palimpsest, the thirteenth century in France being conspicuously a focus of disparate elements. But it had a genuine, living center. Life had achieved a new unity. Men had won a great moral advantage over raw nature in achieving a coherent way of thinking about their experience. They called the general scheme of that experience Christianity, a unified conception of man in relation to God and nature—and the conception was upheld by belief.

We now lack the unity of life. One defect of the Liberal criticism of modern traditionalism is its assumption that traditionists think they "catch" the unity by exposure to evidence of its past existence. The "unity" that Liberals accuse the traditionist of having trifled with is a unity of their own fiction. In the bright light of this perfect, fictitious unity the traditionist looks very silly.

Now among Americans the Southern traditionist is in part a Jeffersonian in so far as he must notice that phase of abstract tradition which is American. Yet, argues the Liberal, how can tradition be Jeffersonian when Jefferson himself was a brilliant star of the eighteenth century Enlightenment, a naturalistic revolution that affected disastrously the doctrine of St. Thomas Aquinas—who is, if anybody is, the very apex of our "tradition"?

The Liberals stretch or trim the traditionist to a fictitious bed, and stand back and say: "Isn't it amazing how uncomfortable he is?" Then they deliver a lecture: You may deny that you don't believe in this fictitious unity, but if you believe that naturalism, progressivism, modernism are false doctrines, then you must *by implication* believe.... But that is Mad Hatter's logic again, in which everything implies in an infinite sorites everything else.

IV

The modern traditionist's reconstruction of history, like the Liberal's, is based upon a naturalistic principle. No living man can exist outside his mental climate. The strictly historical foundations of belief in tradition are the same as the foundations of Liberalism. The "historical method" of recovering the past the traditionist employs, and must employ, no less than the Liberal. And it is a method of viewing our past experience that is deeply involved in the whole naturalistic movement.

But a distinctive feature of the historical method is that

it is negative, or it is at its best neutral. While the view of history as cause and effect, a view that includes the "conditioning" theories of race and climate, has enormously stimulated the scholars' curiosity about the past, the information thus yielded may be arranged in any pattern of belief whatsoever. I may look at English history with John Richard Green as the gradual development of the art of self-government, and I may look at Green as an apologist of nineteenth-century Whiggery and as a father of the Liberals. I may look at English history with Hilaire Belloc—as I happen to do with reservations—as the decline of moral standards and human liberty from the twelfth century to our day. Or I may see English history as a bubble in a large cultural process known as *Western Civilization,* and trace out, with Spengler, the "physiognomic" identities of the process with other processes like Chinese culture, or the Magian. For the distinctive feature of the historical method is its technique of studying the past, with historical generalization theoretically ruled out; but because the naturalistic mind thinks and orders according to certain "laws," the laws are read into the past, and thus historical generalization actually functions at high speed. Some kind of pattern or historical picture is necessarily there as a pattern. It is only more or less articulate in different historians.

What the historical method denies, then, is not a logic of history, but rather theories of ultimate value; it actually insists in the long run that the historical picture shall be strictly relative, not that there shall be no picture. So the

conflict between Liberal and traditionist centers first in
the meaning of the historical method itself. The Liberal
may be friendly to tradition while he cannot believe in it.
The traditionist has found in the past a certain unity of
life which he would hand on or create again. The traditionist believes in that unity, on its purely empirical side,
on the same authority to which the Liberal appeals in dis-
believing in it. Both appeal to the findings of history.
Both, equipped with the historical method, construct a
relativist pattern of reference. But the Liberal, as a relativist, denies the validity of absolutes even in those ages
that thought they were living by them. The traditionist,
who is also a modernist and inevitably a relativist in procedure, and, as I think, a more thorough skeptic than the
Liberal, includes in his historical picture absolute beliefs
as being implicit and emergent in experience at all times,
and under certain conditions, explicit and realized. And
here it is the traditionist's historical sense that tells him
that this must be so: men in other times have lived by
absolutes, and although he himself does not now live by
absolutes, he is convinced, partly on the evidence of the
historical method that he shares with the Liberal, that
man needs absolute beliefs in order con pletely to realize
his nature.

What Liberal historian, who understands the profoundly relative ground of his procedure, can logically
contest this even more extreme extension of his skepticism? For the genuine skeptic will allow for the possibility
of faith; otherwise there is the faith of unbelief. Under

relativism the very structure of history is relative—which means that so long as the system is not closed it may include all potentialities. It has as a matter of fact included them all—all but absolutes. For the meaning of relativism in history is that it allows us to believe anything that we want to believe—as the late Sir J. G. Frazer believed that every time an animal appeared in primitive societies it meant totemism.

V

Opponents of tradition accuse the traditionist of using a capital T—of making a quality an abstraction and an absolute. This is the assumption of the Liberals. It is a curious kind of absolute for the Liberals to construct, and in most of them it is doubtless only a debater's absolute that puts the traditionist in the wrong. The traditionist has never had tradition lying about him in lumps, nor hanging luxuriantly from the trees. Tradition is not an object of belief. It is a quality of judgment and of conduct, rooted in a concrete way of life, that demands constant rediscovery; and it must be maintained with the hardest vigilance.

The question: What is tradition? is unanswerable. It is not a *thing*. The proper question is: What qualities of our experience at a given time are worth preserving? For tradition is quite simply that quality of life that we have got from our immediate past, or if we are makers of tradition, the quality that we create and try to pass on to the next generation. If we are already traditional persons, we shall pass on something that we did not make, but in the act of transmitting it we submit it to the hazard of change and expect it to be altered and renewed in the moral problems of the future. It has been the privilege of every generation to decide for or against tradition—to decide whether it shall continue to live within a fundamental unity of morals that it has received from the immediate past.

Today no American community can transmit a tradition whole. If the future shall have one, we have got to make it. For with respect to tradition only three kinds of society are possible. There is the anti-traditional society— or call it, if you will, culture—which destroys the tradition and produces the un-traditional society that we have today. The anti-traditional society or culture agitated for its ends from the beginning of the Industrial Revolution to the Great War, when it triumphed, and passed into the untraditional state in which the choice, for the ordinary man, between tradition and disorder ceased to exist. The untraditional society then is one in which the moral unity of man is no longer an issue. Having rejected a social and economic structure that makes possible free decision in the moral sense, we live in a system of money references that the moral will cannot control: for the institution of controlled property we have substituted finance-capitalism, which is the creation of nineteenth-century foreign trade and industrialism.

The traditional society is based upon property, and

property means not only ownership but control; not only economic privilege but moral obligation; not only rights but duties; not only material welfare but moral standards. And property means all this because the joint fact of ownership-control resides in the human character and is commensurate with human character. Finance-capitalism is ownership apart from human character because it is ownership apart from control; moral agency becomes, under this system, economic purpose, and we get, in place of Christian or Moral Man, Economic Man, a living abstraction who is necessarily abstract, being the mere expression of another abstraction—Economic Productiveness. Economic Man is controlled by his system of production; the man of property controls his system of production. The Economic Man wields the science of the mastery of nature; man in the culture of property adds to the science of nature his mastery of the science, the excess of attention and love that is art, which is the symbol of man's mastery of himself.

A society based upon property will pass on its heritage in a concrete form, and this concrete form, property, which means moral control of the means of life, is the medium in which tradition is passed on. The traditional society will envisage its heritage in moral terms because its members must be personally responsible for the material basis of life. A society personally responsible for the material basis of life is a traditional society. Such a society is any community of men who pass to the next generation, under a definite conception of human nature, a code of conduct;

and this code of conduct, apart from its utility, is a symbol of the excess of attention and love which is art and religion—a proof that men have mastered not only a productive process but themselves as well. They are able to act humanly and not merely economically towards the material basis of life and towards one another.

In our own un-traditional society there is a vast hiatus between the successful operation of the "means of production" and coherent moral standards. Individuals here and there maintain standards. But there is no code of conduct, no mature articulation of the code in religion, that is commensurate with the economic process. A traditional society not only makes possible, but actually enjoins, the affirmation of a high code that permeates every phase of public and private experience.

A society dominated by its economics is bound to be composed chiefly of men, whether workers or capitalists, to whom "making a living" and a "way of life" are quite different pursuits. Both workers and capitalists are operating the means of production without controlling it. The capitalist class seeks a realm of moral choice apart from its livelihood—and we get American culture today, a meaningless collection of other peoples' arts and morals, meaningless because irrelevant to the material basis of life. But the traditional community is made up of men who are never quite making their living and who never quite cease to make it: they are making their living all the time and affirming their code all the time. In societies dominated by the moral and religious view, the life of men and their livelihood approximate a unity in which to speak of the one is to speak of the other.

These qualities seem to me to be the essentials of "tradition." And we are wasting our time if we suppose that St. Thomas, religious authority, the Catholic Church, were more than approximations of a moral ideal by certain men at certain times under certain conditions. It is a special "psychosis" of modern man that impels him to "restore the past." Those ages of the past that he cries for had restored nothing whatever: they created something, and although they levied upon the past, they quickly transformed their borrowings, and amalgamated past and present into a whole.

VI

The problem of belief involved in the traditional view is peculiarly difficult because an irrelevance clouds it. The real problem is not religious authority or our ability to restore the Middle Ages or Old South, nor yet whether Jefferson as a Rationalist was not hostile to tradition. We have got first of all to answer a question. What ground is there for belief in the value of the moral unity of man—the unity of moral choice and material occupation? The answer is: Every ground. That is an absolute upon which all men are united, the relativist historian no less than the Dominican priest—the historian joining in an affirmation that his occupation on principle denies.

The belief that moral unity is desirable is not a belief

that it is automatically possible: that is the irrelevance set up by the anti-traditionist to befog the issue. I think it is worth repeating that the future realization of a traditional society of morally unified persons is not an object of belief; it is or it is not a potentiality of fact that no one can predict. But the belief in moral unity as the highest good that men can seek to achieve waits upon no question of fact. It is a belief inherent in our experience, not only in individual experience, but in the experience of our civilization as we recover it from history. If we see it only as an historical generalization, there is even from that point of view as much ground for belief in it as there is for its antithesis—in which no man, living or dead, has ever believed.

Examine the antithesis: *Moral disunity is desirable.* It violates a fundamental assumption of all men as profoundly as an undistributed middle destroys an Aristotelian syllogism.

Since the value of moral unity is a kind of *a priori* truth, the anti-traditionist, attempting to undermine his opponent's position, must question, not this truth, but the kind of medium that the traditionist sets up for its realization. For whether the unity itself is desirable or undesirable is an imperative of reference, as absolute as Pascal's wager; and to it we must submit all our experience.

At a particular stage of traditional life in Europe one expression of its moral unity was the worship of the Virgin at Chartres—just as the unity was an expression of that worship. When a peasant plowed a field he did not cease to worship the Virgin, nor at the altar did he cease to be a plowman. The plowman, of course, living unreflectingly in the medieval scheme, made no distinction between imperative of reference and imperative of belief; yet had he rejected belief he could not have escaped the dilemma, unity or disunity, as an imperative of reference.

Nor can the modern Liberal escape that reference. When the Liberal says that he believes in "progressivism" because it has triumphed, he is saying that he cannot believe in unity because we have disunity. He cannot believe in truth because we are dominated by falsehood. He is affirming his loyalty to a program in which he not only *does* not believe, but cannot, on the grounds that he offers, believe; nor can any one else believe in progressivism on the mere ground of its "success." When the Liberal backs off from tradition because he cannot believe in it, because "it is not a question of what one feels one needs to believe, but simply of what one can believe," he is confusing with belief the potentiality of fact. He is saying that in order to believe in the value of traditional life—the life of moral unity that can be handed on—we have got first to know that it will be handed on. The validity of the traditional program, for the Liberal positivist, is the sheer accident of its future success.

Now this brings us, I think, back to the first section of this essay—to the positivist's discovery that the "behavioristic reference" of belief *is* the belief. Belief is not our way of thinking about what we do, for that is rationalization; it is what we *do* that defines what we "really" believe. A young man is writing a poem. He is not really writing a poem; he is trying to justify himself in a difficult social maladjustment in which the ordinary forms of social justification have been unsuccessfully tried or are too difficult. There is no quarrel with this view—so long as it is applied strictly to the modern mind suffering from disunity and about which the theory is descriptively true.

The positivist procedure not only implies its appropriate theory of disunity; it has risen upon the modern experience of disunity. There is no space here to go into the implications of this procedure. It becomes profoundly unhistorical when it argues, as it often does argue, that the medieval plowman was rationalizing his hard labor with worship of the Virgin at Chartres: the historian reads into the past his own moral disunity. He is saying that the material medium of life must be forever impregnable to moral control, that the medieval plowman's labor was identical with the machine-tending of the modern factory worker, who has no moral control over the means of livelihood because he lacks all moral connection with it. The historian, in effect, tells us that the moral unification of human purpose and material medium has never been achieved, cannot be achieved, and so never will be achieved; and that it is a delusion.

And he is right—if we allow him to deal, as he usually does, irresponsibly with his fictitious absolutes. For the perfect traditional society has never existed, can never exist, and is a delusion. But the perfect traditional society as an imperative of reference—not as an absolute lump to be

measured and weighed—has always existed and will continue to haunt the moral imagination of man. Whether
the modern mechanical society can be brought to a state
of mechanical perfection yet remains to be seen; but as a
logical absolute it can be envisaged by the scientific mind.
The traditional society cannot be envisaged as a mechanical, scientific absolute, and that is why the modern Liberal
historian, erecting it into a fictitious absolute that we have
seen, can easily discredit it.

But the traditional procedure is in the long run less
vaultingly ambitious. It aims at no mechanical perfection,
no natural absolute; it does not attempt to abstract the
material process from the moral whole of life. The traditionist attempts only what the sculptor attempts to do with
his stone—to bring his experience to form and order.

In modern societies, which are rapidly moving through
finance-capitalism toward collectivism—the archetype of
the un-traditional life—the means of livelihood are more
and more divorced from the moral agency of men. Maxim
Gorky said: "We have liberated men from the burden of
property." In Western societies we too are separating the
moral nature of man from the primary fact of his existence
—his livelihood. Our ideas about ourselves thus become
rationalizations, and are chaotic and irresponsible. But in
an absolute imperative of reference, we must construct a
moral picture of ourselves; it is a necessity that we cannot
deny. Our moral picture will be good or bad, but it cannot
cease to be. Our modern moral pictures have no organic
relation to what we are doing; our moral life has lost its

hold upon our material life. In the effort to understand our conduct we commit ourselves to rationalizations—pictures of conduct irrelevant to what we actually do.

So the modern positivist technique is profoundly relevant to our experience: our moral beliefs about ourselves are profoundly irrelevant to our experience. And the Liberal may well stand appalled at the futility of our modern beliefs. But then we may ask: "How can he continue to think that he believes in them?" He will answer: "On the ground of their success"—whatever kind of belief success may be.

WHAT IS A TRADITIONAL
SOCIETY?[1]

NOT LONG ago, I hope with no sinister purpose, I used the word tradition before a group of Southern men who had met to discuss the problems of the South. A gentleman from North Carolina rose; he said that tradition was meaningless, and he moved that we drop the word. I have a certain sympathy with that view. Many features of our lives that we call traditions are meaningless; we confuse with tradition external qualities which are now, in our rich American middle class, mere stage properties of a way of life that can no longer be lived. For the stage-set differs from the natural scene, I take it, in offering us a conventional surface without depth, and the additional facility of allowing us to stand before it on Saturday and Sunday and to resume, on Monday, the real business of life. Tradition as we see it today has little to do with the real business of life; at best it can make that grim reality two-sevenths less grim—if indeed the pretense of our weekend traditionalists is not actually grimmer than the reality they apologetically prefer but from which they desire, part of the time, to escape.

1 The Phi Beta Kappa Address at the University of Virginia, June, 1936.

I do not understand this romanticism, and I bring it to your attention because, here within the walls of Mr. Jefferson's University, there is a special tradition of realism in thinking about the nature of tradition. The presiding spirit of that tradition was clear in his belief that the way of life and the livelihood of men must be the same; that the way we make our living must strongly affect the way of life; that our way of getting a living is not good enough for us if we are driven by it to pretend that it is something else; that we cannot pretend to be landed gentlemen two days of the week if we are middle-class capitalists the five others. You will remember Ruskin's objection to the Gothic factory-architecture of his age—the ornamentation he suggested for the cornices of a kind of building that was new in that time. Ruskin's stylized money-bags set at the right rhythmic intervals around the cornices of the Bethlehem Steel Corporation might be symbolic of something going on inside, but I think the Chairman of the Board would rightly object that Ruskin was not a good satirist, but merely a sentimentalist; and the Chairman would leave his cornices bare. Yet, while the Chairman of the Board might be committed on the one hand to an economic realism, he might on the other indulge himself in softer materials in another direction; he might buy or build a Georgian mansion somewhere near Middleburg, Virginia, and add to it—if they were not already there— the correct row of columns that Mr. Jefferson adapted to Virginia after a visit to the Maison Carré at Nîmes.

Mr. Jefferson could not know Ruskin, but he knew

about medieval Europe, and he disliked it. He never visited Mr. Walpole at Strawberry Hill, but I wish he had. He would have rejoiced that Walpole's week-end Gothic —if you will allow the anachronism for the sake of the moral—meant the final destruction, in England, of the Middle Ages. He would have known that to revive something is to hasten its destruction—if it is only picturesquely and not sufficiently revived. For the moment the past becomes picturesque it is dead. I do not agree with Mr. Jefferson about the Middle Ages, but I surmise that he would have considered a revival of the past very much in this light. He himself was trying to revive the small freeholder who had been dispossessed by the rising capitalist of the eighteenth century.

Now one of the curious features of our mentality since the Renaissance is the historical imagination. No other civilization, I believe, has had this gift. I use the term not in a strict sense, but in a very general sense, and perhaps not in a wholly good sense. I mean that with the revival of Greek studies men in Europe began to pose as Greeks. After a couple of centuries, when the pose, too heroic to last, grew tired, they posed as Romans of the Republic. There we have a nice historical dramatization of the common sense of the eighteenth century. We on this side of the Atlantic were not unaffected by it. There is evidence that our Revolutionary fathers were the noblest Romans of them all. There is certainly not a Virginian, nor a Southerner of Virginian ancestry, whose great-great-grandfather did not write letters to his son in the style of Addison, a vehicle nicely fitted to convey the matter of Cicero. *Libidinosa enim et intemperans adulescentia effetum corpus tradit senectuti*—it is not from the orations, but the rhythm and sentiment here were the model of the *ore orotundo* style that dominated society in the South and other parts of America for three generations. Those generations, if our records of their more elegant representatives do not lie, were not much impressed with the ravages of youthful license upon the body, which, as Cicero has just told us, passes wearily into old age. The young blade of Albemarle of 1770, sitting over a punch-bowl in the tavern after a day of Cicero with the learned Parson Douglas, was not, at that moment, an examplar of Cicero's morals, but I suspect that his conversation, even after the bottom of the bowl began to be visible, retained a few qualities of the Ciceronian style.

The style is the point of a digression that I hope you will not think frivolous. I hold no brief for Cicero—he is a dull mind in any language—but I do hold that the men of the early American Republic had a profound instinct for high style, a genius for dramatizing themselves at their own particular moment of history. They were so situated economically and politically that they were able to form a definite conception of their human role: they were not ants in an economic ant-hill, nor were they investigating statistically the behavior of other ants. They knew what they wanted because they knew what they, themselves, were. They lived in a social and economic system that permitted them to develop a human character that functioned in every level of life, from the economic process to the county horse-race.

The Virginian of the 1790's might have found a better dramatic part than that of the Roman in *toga virilis*—as Mr. Custis, the first Southern dilettante, liked to paint him—but it was the easiest role to lay hold upon at that time, and it was distinctly better than no imaginative version of himself at all. A few years ago Mr. T. S. Eliot told an audience at this University that there are two kinds of mythology, a higher and a lower. The Roman *toga* of our early Republic was doubtless of a kind of lower mythology, inferior to the higher mythology of the Christian thirteenth century, and I suppose Mr. Eliot would prefer the higher vision, as I myself should were I allowed a preference. But we must remember that the rationalism of the eighteenth century had made myths of all ranks exceedingly scarce, as the romantic poets were beginning to testify; yet the Virginian did remarkably well with the minor myth that his age permitted him to cultivate. Mr. Custis's paintings may seem to us to be afflicted with a sort of aesthetic giantism, and his blank-verse dramas, in which every hero is an alabaster Washington named Marcus Tullius Scipio Americanus, are unreadable today. They must have been a kind of inexquisite torture even when they were written. But Mr. Custis built Arlington, and Arlington is something to have built. He could not have built it, of course, if Mr. Jefferson had not first built a house upon a place that I believe is locally called the Little Mountain; but then Mr. Jefferson could not have built Monticello had he not been dominated by the lower myth of the *toga virilis*.

Perhaps this lower myth, from whatever source it may come—Rome, Greece, the age of Cellini, the naturalism of the South Seas, or even the Old South—this little myth is a figment of the historical imagination, that curious faculty of Western men that I have already mentioned. The men of our early Republic were powerfully endowed in this faculty. It is not the same as a religion, if by religion we mean Christianity in the Middle Ages; nor is it the same as the religious imagination under any conceivable culture, for the religious imagination is timeless and unhistoric. The minor myth is based upon ascertainable history.

There is a chart that we might look at for a moment, but only for a moment; I offer it not as history, but as a device to ease the strain of the idea of traditional society that I am trying to give in so short a space. First, there is the religious imagination, which can mythologize indiscriminately history, legend, trees, the sea, animals, all being humanly dramatized, somehow converted to the nature of man. Secondly, there is the historical imagination, which is the religious imagination *manqué*—an exercise of the myth-making propensity of man within the restricted realm of historical event. Men see themselves in the stern light of the character of Cato, but they can no longer see themselves under the control of a tutelary deity. Cato actually lived; Apollo was merely far-darting.

The third stage is the complete triumph of positivism. And with the complete triumph of positivism, in our own time, we get, in place of so workable a makeshift as the historical imagination, merely a truncation of that phrase in which the adjective has declared its independence. It has set up for a noun. Under positivism we get just plain, everyday history. If this is an obscure conception, I must hasten to say that although history cannot write itself, although it must be written by men whose minds are as little immune to prejudice as to the law of contradiction, it is true that any sort of creative imagination is, on principle, eliminated. Yet in recognition of history's impotence to bring itself into being, the historians give us a new word: method. We live in the age of the historical method. Method brings history into being.

I shall not labor the point here, but I do think it is fair to say that *history,* although it has become attached to *method,* is still a noun of agency, as the grammarians call it, trying to do its own work. I think this is true simply because on principle scientific *method* is itself not attached to anything. It is just abstract method—from which plain, abstract, inhuman history differs not by a hair. Of course, I am talking about the historian's ideal of physical law— his belief that history must conform to the ideal of a normative science, whether or not it can mean anything written that way. The historical method then may be briefly described—by one who does not believe in its use— as the way of discovering historical "truths" that are true in some other world than that inhabited by the historian and his fellow men: truths, in a word, that are true for the historical method.

Now most of you have read *The Waste Land,* but I shall ask you to hear a passage from it again for the sake of those who have not read it:

> *The Chair she sat in, like a burnished throne*
> *Glowed on the marble, where the glass*
> *Held up by standards wrought with fruited vines*
> *From which a golden Cupidon peeped out*
> *(Another hid his eyes behind his wing)*
> *Doubled the flames of seven-branched candelabra*
> *Reflecting light upon the table as*
> *The glitter of her jewels rose to meet it*
> *From satin cases poured in rich profusion;*
> *In vials of ivory and colored glass*
> *Unstoppered, lurked her strange synthetic perfumes.*

In this handsome *décor* the lady, I imagine, is about to dress for dinner. On the walls and ceiling are scenes from an heroic past:

> *Huge sea-wood fed with copper*
> *Burned green and orange, framed by the colored*
>   *stone,*
> *In which sad light a carvèd dolphin swam.*
> *Above the antique mantel was displayed*
> *As though a window gave upon the sylvan scene*
> *The change of Philomel, by the barbarous king*
> *So rudely forced; yet there the nightingale*
> *Filled all the desert with inviolable voice....*

People living in such favorable influences, partaking of
the best of our history and of the art of the great tradition,
command our most interested attention: they will at least
exhibit the benefits of a good lower mythology. We may
expect them to show us, if not the innocence of the religious imagination, a high style that expresses, or is the
expression of, the walls that we have just looked at. But
no; the poet warns us as follows:

> *And other withered stumps of time*
> *Were told upon the walls; staring forms*
> *Leaned out, leaning, hushing the room en-*
> *   closed.*
> *Footsteps shuffled on the stair.*

I hope you will forgive me if I venture to think that the
shuffling feet are about to bring into the room the historical method. For, after some desperately aimless conversation, in which both the woman and the man seem to
feel little but a bored exhaustion and vacuity of purpose,
the woman suddenly says:

> *"What shall I do now? What shall I do?*
> *"I shall rush out as I am, and walk the street*
> *"With my hair down, so. What shall we do to-*
> *   morrow?*
> *"What shall we ever do?"*

Her companion replies—and I ask you to place what he
says against the heroic background of Renaissance art on

the ceiling and walls: what he says does reduce it, I think, to withered stumps of time:

> *The hot water at ten.*
> *And if it rains, a closed car at four.*
> *And we shall play a game of chess,*
> *Pressing lidless eyes, and waiting for a*
> *knock upon the door.*

Now fortunately upon this occasion I am neither poet nor literary critic. Here I am a moralist, and if I find more to my use in Mr. Eliot's poem than he would willingly allow, you will remember that moralists these days are desperate persons, and must in their weaker moments squeeze a moral even out of modern poetry. If the chess game seems trivial as a symbol of aimless intellectuality, its intention is nevertheless just. The rich experience of the great tradition depicted in the room receives a violent shock in contrast with a game that symbolizes the inhuman abstraction of the modern mind. In proposing the game of chess the man is proposing an exercise in a kind of truth that has no meaning for either of them. The woman in this remarkable scene has just said that she can think of nothing to do—the moralist would gloss that as lack of purpose—and she intends to rush out into the street with her hair down.

What does this mean? It means that in ages which suffer the decay of manners, religion, morals, codes, our indestructible vitality demands expression in violence and chaos; it means that men who have lost both the higher myth of religion and the lower myth of historical dramatization have lost the forms of human action; it means that they are no longer capable of defining a human objective, of forming a dramatic conception of human nature; it means that they capitulate from their human role to a series of pragmatic conquests which, taken alone, are true only in some other world than that inhabited by men.

The woman in Mr. Eliot's poem is, I believe, the symbol of man at the present time. He is surrounded by the grandeurs of the past, but he does not participate in them; they do not sustain him. To complete the allegory, the man represents a kind of truth that I have described in very general terms as the historical method: he offers us the exercise of intellect to no purpose, a game that we cannot relate to our conduct, an instrument of power over both past and present which we can neither control nor properly use.

Man in this plight lives in an untraditional society. For an untraditional society does not permit its members to pass to the next generation what it received from its immediate past. Why is this so? I have tried to describe in moral terms some of the defects of life in an untraditional society—and I expect merely to ask, and not to answer, whether there is not some kind of analysis that we may subject our situation to, that will show us one way of understanding the fundamental difference between tradition and non-tradition?

I shall return to a question that I asked in the begin-

ning. Why do many modern people live one kind of life
five days a week and another the two other days? Why is
it that a middle-class capitalist from Pittsburgh or Bir-
mingham desires an ante-bellum Georgian house near Lex-
ington, Kentucky, or Middleburg, Virginia? And why was
it that the men who built those houses desired only those
houses, and made serious objections in the eighteen-sixties
to being forcibly removed from them? There are many
answers to these questions, but I have space for only one.
The middle-class capitalist does not believe in the dignity
of the material basis of his life; his human nature demands
a homogeneous pattern of behavior that his economic life
will not give him. He doubtless sees in the remains of the
Old South a symbol of the homogeneous life. But the ante-
bellum man saw no difference between the Georgian house
and the economic basis that supported it. It was all of one
piece.

I am exaggerating, but permit me the exaggeration so
that I may make this matter as clear as I can. Man has
never achieved a perfect unity of his moral nature and his
economics; yet he has never failed quite so dismally in that
greatest of all human tasks as he is failing now. Ante-
bellum man, in so far as he achieved a unity between his
moral nature and his livelihood, was a traditional man.
He dominated the means of life; he was not dominated
by it. I think the distinguishing feature of a traditional
society is simply that. In order to make a livelihood men
do not have to put aside their moral natures. Traditional
men are never quite making their living, and they never

quite cease to make it. Or put otherwise: they are making their living all the time, and affirming their humanity all the time. The whole economic basis of life is closely bound up with moral behavior, and it is possible to behave morally all the time. It is this principle that is the center of the philosophy of Jefferson.

Yet what is there traditional about this? The answer is that if such a society could come into being now, and had no past whatever, it would be traditional because it could hand something on. That something would be a moral conception of man in relation to the material of life. The material basis of life, in such a society, is not hostile to the perpetuation of a moral code, as our finance-capitalist economics unquestionably is. It is an old story by this time that our modern economic system can be operated efficiently regardless of the moral stature of the men who operate it.

The kind of property that sustains the traditional society is not only *not* hostile to a unified moral code; it is positively the basis of it. Moreover it is the medium, just as canvas is the medium of a painter, through which that code is passed to the next generation. For traditional property in land was the primary medium through which man expressed his moral nature; and our task is to restore it or to get its equivalent today. Finance-capitalism, a system that has removed men from the responsible control of the means of a livelihood, is necessarily hostile to the development of a moral nature. Morality is responsibility to a given set of conditions. The further the modern system develops in the direction that it has taken for two generations, the more anti-traditional our society will become, and the more difficult it will be to pass on the fragments of the traditions that we inherit.

The higher myth of religion, the lower myth of history, even ordinary codes of conduct, cannot preserve themselves; indeed they do not exist apart from our experience. Since the most significant feature of our experience is the way we make our living, the economic basis of life is the soil out of which all the forms, good or bad, of our experience must come.